STILL IN LOVE WITH YOU

STILL IN LOVE WITH YOU

The Story of Hank and Audrey Williams

Lycrecia Williams
Dale Vinicur

RUTLEDGE HILL PRESS
Nashville, Tennessee

Copyright ©1989 Lycrecia Williams Hoover and Dale Vinicur

Jacket photograph courtesy of Schofield Photographers. Nashville, Tennessee.

Published in Nashville, Tennessee, by Rutledge Hill Press 211 Seventh Avenue North, Nashville, Tennessee 37219

Typography by Bailey Typography, Nashville, Tennessee

Library of Congress Cataloging-in-Publication Data

Williams, Lycrecia, 1941–
    Still in love with you : the story of Hank and Audrey Williams / Lycrecia Williams, Dale Vinicur.
        p. cm.
    ISBN 1-55853-048-7
    1. Williams, Hank, 1923–1953. 2. Country musicians—United States—Biography. 3. Williams, Audrey, 1923-1975. 4. Musicians' wives—Biography. I. Vinicur, Dale, 1945– . II. Title.
ML420.W55W47 1989
782.42164'2'092—dc20   89-37030
[B]   CIP
                                                                               MN

Printed in the United States of America
3 4 5 6 7 8 — 97

I wish to dedicate this book to the thousands of people who were, and still are, the fans of my mother and father, Audrey and Hank Williams. I hope that everyone who reads this story will better understand Mother and Daddy. A child could not have had better parents to love them than I had. They taught me so much.

I would also like to make a special dedication to my two closest friends, Delila Ellis and Carla Norrell. I have drawn enormous strength from them, when my mother passed away and at other critical times. Delila and Carla, you both shall always be in my heart and in my thoughts.

Contents

Preface

I want to start this book by saying that Hank Williams was not my blood father. I never knew that man. He left before I was born. Mother married Hank when I was three years old, and from the time I was about two, he was just always around. He bought my clothes, paid my doctor bills, carried me to school, and gave me a home, love, and understanding. To me that's being a father. Hank Williams was as much my father as anyone could ever be. I called him Daddy, and I loved him very much. And he loved me.

I wrote this book because I needed to put the pieces together about my parents. I wanted to make sense out of what I could remember and what I read in all the books and articles and even song lyrics about Mother and Daddy.

As I started putting down my memories, I had to ask some other people what they recalled about a particular time or event. Some of these people aren't well known, but they all shared some important times with Mother and Daddy, and I learned things I had never heard before or was too young to remember.

I knew I'd come up on the pain again. There's no way around it when you know that the two people who loved you most as a child wound up destroying themselves, one after the other and in the very same way. But there were laughs and good times, too, and those memories are the strongest of all. I know Mother and Daddy loved me, and I know they loved each other right up to the end.

Introduction

I first met Lycrecia in the summer of 1986. Her family home on Franklin Road in Nashville had just been reconstructed on Music Row, and she was serving as hostess. As a country music fan, I was familiar with her father's life story and music and already loved and admired him. I knew very little about Audrey, Hank's wife and Lycrecia's mother, however, except for the unflattering descriptions of her as a nagging, ambitious, cold-hearted bitch that I had read in the various books written about Hank. From the first time that I met Lycrecia, though, I knew that something was missing from everything I had read or heard about Audrey Williams. Lycrecia is a very dignified lady; she's also friendly, honest, and down-to-earth. I feel sure that she must have acquired those qualities from the parents who raised her.

As we grew to be friends, Lycrecia talked freely about her family — of her happy childhood and the deep love her mother and father had for their children and each other. We also talked of the sadness of her parents' divorce and both of their deaths, nearly twenty-three years apart, from the ravages of alcoholism. It was incredible to me that no previous biographer of Hank Williams had given more than passing attention to Lycrecia. Hank, Jr., was just a baby when his father died, and Audrey herself had died in 1975. So only Lycrecia, who was nearly twelve when her daddy passed away, could recall firsthand the details of the Williams family's private lives and how they all were affected by Hank's sudden rise to stardom and the tragedies that followed. As we talked, month after month, I became convinced that the real story of Hank and Audrey Williams had never been told. Hank's depth of character had been obscured by legend, and no serious attempt had ever been made to understand Audrey as a person or the complex nature of the relationship between Hank and her. There was also the issue of alcoholism, which so dominated Hank and Audrey's lives — separately and together — that no attempt to tell their story apart from it is possible.

I wanted to leave no stone unturned in my research. I read all of the major and minor books ever written about Hank Williams. My favorite was a short work by Hank's best-known fiddler, Jerry Rivers, called *Hank Williams, from Life to Legend*, which concentrated on the Nashville years. Roger Williams' (no relation) *Sing a Sad Song* contains a lot of information about Hank's early life, as do two interesting, homespun pamphlets published separately by the communities of Georgiana and Greenville, Alabama, where Hank spent most of his childhood. Another biography, *Hank Williams, Country Music's Tragic King*, by Jay Caress, also explores Hank's early years and presents a detailed account of his last hours. Bill Koon contributed *Hank Williams, A Bio-Bibliography*, which includes a brief biography, a sketchy discography, and a valuable bibliography of resources on the life of Hank Williams. Chet Flippo wrote a book called *Your Cheatin' Heart*, but his research was very limited and his portrayals of Hank and Audrey are one-dimensional caricatures that have offended everyone who knew and loved them.

In addition to a number of magazine articles located through Bill Koon's bibliography, I carefully examined thirty years of *Billboard* magazine, the *Montgomery Advertiser* from 1937 through 1953, the *Shreveport Times* (Louisiana) for 1948 and 1949, and the *Tennessean* and *Nashville Banner* from 1949 until 1975. A scrapbook of Alabama newspaper clippings provided by Canadian disk jockey and Hank Williams historian Bill MacEwen was of special importance and interest. Information from Audrey's personal papers and memorabilia was helpful, as well. The Alabama Archives in Montgomery and the Country Music Foundation in Nashville were the sites of much of my historical research.

Bob Pinson, principal researcher at the Country Music

Foundation, was invaluable to me in writing this book. Besides being one of the nicest guys in the world, Bob is a true scholar. His Hank Williams discography is the result of many years of careful work, as is an itinerary he has been assembling of Hank's appearance dates throughout his professional career. Both the discography and the itinerary were extremely useful in establishing the chronological and historical accuracy of the book. Bob also acted as historical consultant for *Still in Love with You.*

On the advice of Bernice Turner, a friend of Hank and Audrey's from the early Montgomery days, I read extensively on the subject of alcoholism, including Alcoholic Anonymous' *The Big Book* and *The Dilemma of the Alcoholic Marriage,* Dennis Wholey's *The Courage To Change,* and numerous books on co-dependency, the area of research that explores the problems faced by the families of alcoholics. Bernice told me that Hank and Audrey's story could not be told adequately without an understanding of the disease of alcoholism, and she was absolutely right.

As another important part of my research, I spent many hours in the Davidson County (Nashville) and Montgomery, Alabama, courthouses reconstructing the numerous legal battles that Audrey had faced from the time of Hank's death until the end of her life in 1975. The legal papers collected included birth, death, marriage, and divorce certificates relating to Hank and Audrey, their parents, and their children.

This carefully researched historical structure wouldn't have meant much, however, without the poignant, sensitive, and loving memories of all of the people who were interviewed for the book.

Lycrecia's memories are the backbone of *Still in Love with You,* just as, in her words, "Mother was the backbone of Daddy." She sifted through a lot of years — a lot of painful times — to put her story together. She is a wonderful person, and I will be forever grateful to her for the trust and confidence she put in me from the beginning.

The people we interviewed for this book were, to a person, exceptionally kind and helpful. They all loved Hank and Audrey, Lycrecia, and Hank, Jr., and wanted nothing more for their contributions than a true and heartfelt story. I hope that they will take pride in *Still in Love with You* because it could not have been written without them. Thank you to: Zeke and Helen Clements, Marie Harvell, Flossie Morris, Grant Turner, Dean May, Mac McGee, Goldie Hill and Carl Smith, Buddy Lee, Rena Hailey, Don Helms, Jerry Rivers, Bob McNett, Hillous Butrum, Ronnie Pugh, Bob Pinson, Bob Oermann, Dollie Denny, Kitty Wells and Johnny Wright, Bill and Barbara Koon, Lum York, Wesley Rose, Jud Collins, Erma Williams, Little Jimmy Dickens, Faron Young, Jean Petro, Katie and Ellis Dunn, Bill MacEwen, Dr. Charles Wolfe, Schofield Photographers, Tillman Franks, Bill Monroe, Merle Kilgore, Ruth Garrett, Freda Moon, Mary Clare Rhodes, Loretta and Harold Fleming, Lynette Edwards, Fred Peyser, Murray Nash, Danny Dill, Paul Durham, Doris Davis, Otto Kitsinger, Chet Atkins, Teddy Wilburn, Horace Logan, Bernice Turner, Sam Phillips, Betty Burger, Miss Audrey Ragland, Jean Shepard, Vic Willis, Mr. and Mrs. Leon Harlan, Mack Vickery, John Barnes, Tommy Cash, Frances Preston, Sonny Throckmorton, Ruby Folsom Austin and Cornelia Wallace, Dr. Crawford Adams, Dolores Smiley, Murv Shiner, Marvin and Dot Smythia, Howard White, Goober and Lila Mae Buchanan, Buddy Spicher, Hank Snow, James Neal, Bob Eddings, Dot Robinson, Neal McCormick, Irene and Pete Jones, Homer Bailes, Murrell Stansell, Sr., A. J. Modica, Kyle Cantrell, Billy Walker, Tina Smith, Lindy Leigh, Dolores Bolling, Steve Eng, Braxton and Ola Frances Schuffert, M. C. and Mae Jarrett, Bob McKinnon, Benny Williams, Jean Sopha, Jimmy Goodson, Vic Lewis, Delita Ellis, and X Cosse.

My mother, Rose Biskar, my father, Phil Vinicur, and my brother, Sam Vinicur, have supported me through all the various turns in my life; my beautiful children, Matt and Jason Levy and Gabe Ross, have always loved me despite our family's ups and downs; and my sweet husband, John Janis, is the best.

The experience of writing this book has been one of the high points of my life. Thank you — Lycrecia and everyone else — for your faith and love. I hope I have returned it all ten thousand-fold.

— Dale Vinicur
September 1989

STILL IN LOVE WITH YOU

CHAPTER 1

Daddy's Gone

I was eleven and a half years old at the close of 1952. I spent the night of New Year's Eve with my friends, Mark and Freda Garrett, who were close to my age. The next day, January 1, 1953, we went to the Tennessee Theatre in downtown Nashville to see *April in Paris* with Doris Day and Ray Bolger. Mr. Garrett came and got us in the middle of the movie. As we were walking back out into the lobby, he said, "I came to get you all because, Lycrecia, you've got to go home. They just called and told us that your father has passed away."

I was stunned! I didn't say anything on the way home. I remember they were talking in the car and telling me how sorry they were, but nothing much registered with me.

Mother was in bed when we came in. She was in pretty bad shape, crying and upset. I sat down on the chair next to the bed to talk to her. After a little bit, she said, "Now, Honey, Randall (Hank Jr.) and Miss Ragland (our governess) and I are going down to Montgomery for the funeral. If you want to go, you need to pack your clothes. But if you don't think you want to go, then you can stay with the Garretts until I get back. We won't be gone long." I told her I didn't want to go.

I can't say exactly why I felt that way. I was probably scared and didn't want to see Daddy dead, but I have regretted it since then. I wish Mother had said, "Lycrecia, you need to go pack you some clothes because we've got to go to your Daddy's funeral." I would have probably been upset and cried when I got down there, but it would have helped me accept things

1

better later on. I'm not mad with Mother about it because she was so distraught herself, but I wish she had not given me a choice. By not going I feel that I didn't show Daddy respect. He had always been so good to me.

All the while I stayed with the Garretts, I refused to think about the funeral. I don't think I ever mentioned it. I don't think I brought it up to Mother when she came back. I remember that I did not cry, but I've cried a lot of times since then — for Daddy and, later, for Mother, too.

CHAPTER 2

How's about Saving All Your Time for Me?

In the summer of 1946 when I turned five, I went to live with Mother and Daddy permanently. Before that, I had stayed with Mother's parents, Shelton and Artie Mae Sheppard, on their farm in the Enon community, seven miles from Brundidge, Alabama, population about 1,500, and seven miles from Banks, not much more than a "wide place in the road." Granddaddy's father had built the house we lived in, and Granddaddy, his brothers and sister, his children, and his first grandchild — me — were all born there. Grandmama and Granddaddy were like another mother and father to me. Their youngest daughter, Lynette, was only four years older than I was, and we were raised together like sisters.

My grandparents married on November 23, 1919, and their first child, Audrey Mae (Mother) was born on February 28, 1923. Eldridge was born on August 7, 1926, and Loretta on February 4, 1929. Granddaddy raised cotton, corn, and peanuts, as his father and grandfather had done before him, and also kept hogs, chickens, cows, horses, and mules.

Monthly church services at the Ramer Primitive Baptist Church were important because they brought the people in the community together, and so did the occasional square dances at the homes of local amateur musicians. Granddaddy played a little guitar and fiddle himself, and Mother used to talk about laying in bed as a small child, listening to her daddy plunking away at a few chords on into the night.

3

Mother walked several miles back and forth every day to the Enon grammar school with her brother and sister in a group of about a dozen boys and girls. She felt like she had moved uptown when a big new brick school was built in Banks for grades seven through nine. Mother was a good student, earning As and Bs, but she liked sports and boys better than studying. She dearly loved basketball, and later at Pike County High School in Brundidge, she was the star guard for her team. The school had the number one girls' team in the division for two years.

Sometimes Mother's cousin Katie Ingram would walk home with her after school and stay the night. They would put a mattress on the floor in the dining room, then lie awake half the night laughing and whispering. Mother would confide in Katie her secret desire, to be somebody important, someone famous like a singer or an actress, and have beautiful clothes and a life filled with glamor and excitement.

Loretta remembers that even though her older sister liked nothing better than to dress up and go out, she was also an avid reader and bought paperbacks and magazines from the neighborhood drugstore and borrowed books from the library in Banks. Reading about love and romance and far-off people and places stimulated her imagination.

Mother loved dancing and music, and she studied like a modern teenager, in front of a blaring radio. Her friend Ann Laura recalls, "Audrey would go around and pick up a few friends and take us up to Hucky Berry Hill between Audrey's house and my own. No one lived close by, and Audrey would get in the back of the pick-up truck and say that was her stage. She would place her friends on the truck with her to sing and then have them stop and listen to their echoes. She would say that it was the angels recording their singing. She also said that one day she would be on the 'Grand Ole Opry.'"

Mother herself wrote about an event that shocked and grieved the whole family. "I lost a brother at the age of ten. I was thirteen at the time. I had a premonition or a warning that my little brother was going to die. I can't explain this feeling and I was afraid to tell anyone. I was so young they might have said I was crazy because my brother, Eldridge, was the picture of health. He went fishing with my cousin on a cold, rainy afternoon and came down with double pneumonia and died."

That was on May 1, 1936, and Katie told me about her and Mother going into the woods on the day of the funeral to gather mountain laurel for a bouquet. Eldridge's death seems to have affected Granddaddy harder than anyone else, and he was known to drown his sorrows in an occasional drink or two from that time on.

When a new baby girl was born on September 14, 1938, joy was restored to the grief-stricken family. Mother chose the name Lynette for her new little sister and would always feel like a second mother to her.

Out of the four children, Mother was the only one that Granddaddy ever spanked. She was like him in a lot of ways — headstrong and hot-tempered, but also extremely generous and good-hearted. She was determined that when she wanted to do something she'd just do it, and that caused a certain amount of friction between her and her father.

While still a senior in high school and not quite eighteen, Mother declared her independence by eloping with Erskine Guy, a neighborhood boy she had been dating for a while. She just disappeared one day, and her family was worried sick until they found out where she had gone. Granddaddy was so furious and upset that the newlyweds settled about one hundred and fifty miles away in Gadsden, Alabama, northeast of Birmingham, to keep their distance from him. Loretta remembers it was some time in the winter of 1940–41 when they ran off, but no exact date is known.

By the beginning of summer 1941, however, Mother was back at home, alone and six months pregnant. Erskine had walked off to work one day and never returned. I was born on August 13, 1941, and Erskine Guy is listed as father on my birth certificate, but he never attempted to see or speak with me throughout his life. Mother's 1944 divorce papers cite his "voluntary abandonment" as the reason for the divorce and stipulate support payments. Loretta says Mother never heard from Erskine Guy again after their separation or received one penny of support from him for herself or me, and I believe it.

From the time I was born, it seems that Mother never spoke

of her brief, unhappy marriage and just tried to settle back into life on the farm with her family. Granddaddy and Grandmama were glad to have her back at home, and they bought her a car to prove it, an Oldsmobile. She found work in Brundidge as a drugstore clerk and began to reshape her life.

Mother said nothing exciting had ever happened to her until she met Hank Williams. That's about right, I guess, because the life of an Alabama farm girl is pretty unromantic. She never did like the farm, and I've always thought that the reason she married my biological father was because she wanted to get away from that kind of hard-working life.

I had just turned two when Mother and Daddy met. Mother described their first encounter in her unfinished memoirs:

> It was the late summer of 1943 that I first met a tall, skinny, part Indian, brown-eyed man named Hank Williams. He had a guitar strung around his neck and was playing a medicine show in Banks, Alabama, my little hometown.
>
> My dad's only sister, Ethel, and I were passing through Banks on the way to a club in another little town, Troy, Alabama. My aunt noticed a crowd of people gathered around a makeshift stage on the back of an old house trailer. A show was in full swing and we stopped to watch it. We sat there to listen, and pretty soon Hank came on and sang. At this time I had never heard of him, but lots of people down there had because of his fifteen-minute radio shows on WSFA in Montgomery which reached all over that area. I knew then. Something told me when I first heard Hank that someday he would be number one.
>
> At intermission, the emcee walked over to the microphone and started giving a hard sales pitch about his herbs, etc., that would cure anything wrong with a person. The entertainers started passing among the crowd peddling the cure-all medicine for fifty cents a bottle. Some of the people were standing and some were sitting in their cars, as my aunt and I were. When Hank came by my car, he had a bottle of herbs and said, "Ma'am, don't you think you need . . ." He just kind of glanced and looked back, did a doubletake, and said "No, ma'am, I don't believe you do." I'll never forget that expression on his face and the way he looked straight at me. He sounded so country, too. I was barely nineteen years old and pretty shy back in those days.
>
> At this point my aunt piped in and said, "Audrey and I are going down to this club in Troy. Would you like to go with us?"

He said, "Yes, ma'am, I would if you'll just wait until I do the next show." She told him we'd wait and we did, and that's what started the whole thing. We had fun that night, and when we dropped Hank back by the trailer, he asked me if I would pick him up the following day since he didn't have a car. I said that I would.

When I arrived the next day about noontime, I couldn't believe my eyes. Hank appeared in the trailer doorway and walked over to my car. He looked like a tramp. He was unshaven, his hair was standing up on end, he was in his bare feet with no shirt, and slightly intoxicated. I wanted to drive away but he opened the door, sat down and said, "Ma'am, I want to talk to you." I told him I couldn't go anywhere with him in that condition. He asked me please to wait for him to get cleaned up. He looked so pitiful I decided to wait and hear him out.

We drove around most of the afternoon. During the course of our ride, I gave him plenty of black coffee and tomato juice. He told me how at the age of fourteen he and a guy named Hezzy Adair got together and called themselves Hank and Hezzy, and they worked as a team for a short time. Then he formed his own group and called them the Drifting Cowboys. He had an early morning radio show on WSFA in Montgomery, and he could advertise on the show where he and the Drifting Cowboys would be performing. Most of the time, it was at schoolhouses or small honky-tonks. He drifted along like this for three to four years with musicians quitting and new ones coming in.

Then, with a faraway look in his eyes, he said, "To tell you the truth, I drank too much and the radio station let me go. So here I am working on a medicine show. There's something else I want to tell you," he added, "but I can't now." I was anxious to know what it was, but I wouldn't push it.

That night after the show, actually my second date with Hank, he asked me to marry him. He proposed by saying, "I know you're gonna think I'm crazy, but will you meet me in Troy tomorrow and marry me?" I thought, the man has to be completely out of his mind, never dreaming . . .

❖   ❖   ❖   ❖   ❖

I'm free and ready so we can go steady,
How's about savin' all your time for me.
No more lookin', I know I've been tooken,
How's about keepin' steady company.

❖   ❖   ❖   ❖   ❖

I wish Mother had written more. I'd like to hear what she had to say about the time between that first proposal and the day they actually married on December 15, 1944. And I wish I had talked to Daddy more about his family and his life before he met Mother. What I know about those times has come to me from family members on both sides as well as musicians in Daddy's early bands.

At the time Mother and Daddy met, he was living in Montgomery at his mother's boardinghouse. His mother, Lillie Stone, stood nearly six feet tall and was a strong and fearless woman. She had married her first husband and Daddy's father, Lon Williams, on November 12, 1916, in Butler County, Alabama, only about one hundred miles west of Banks. Their daughter Irene was born on August 8, 1922, and Hiram (Daddy) just a year later on September 17, 1923. For the next six years, Lon and Lillie moved their family from community to community, seeking financial stability and hoping to settle down.

Then, when Daddy was only six years old, his father entered the veteran's hospital in Biloxi, Mississippi, where he stayed for nearly a decade. An old World War I injury had caused an aneurism to form near his brain, and it eventually paralyzed his face and affected his speech. He did recover many years later, but his wife had already divorced him by then and his children barely remembered their father.

Facing the Depression years without a man in the family was tough, but Mrs. Stone (Lillie Williams then) had learned to be enterprising. She opened her first roominghouse in Georgiana when Daddy was about seven and taught her son and daughter to earn a few extra pennies after school. Daddy bagged peanuts and sold them on the street, shined shoes, ran errands, and did any other odd jobs he could find. They were poor, but no one had anything back then.

Mrs. Stone played the organ at the Mt. Olive West Baptist Church when Daddy was small. She was proud of her young son who stood on the bench beside her and sang the gospel songs along with the rest of the congregation.

I have been told that Daddy was a frail, skinny, spirited child with a serious side that grew more pronounced after his father left. He must have been a lonely and confused little boy about the time he met up with a kindly old black street musician from nearby Greenville named Rufe Payne, or TeeTot, as he was called. TeeTot probably introduced Daddy to the basics of singing the blues, picking a guitar, and entertaining a crowd. Daddy must have been attracted to music and performing right away, because he soon began to spend as much time as he could at the local musicians' hangouts, Cade Durham's shoe shop and Jim Warren's Jewelry and Instrument Store. In 1933, when hard times forced the Williams family to move the few miles north to Greenville, Daddy had even more access to his old friend TeeTot who lived near the railroad tracks.

Unfortunately, Daddy got introduced to something else at this early age — drinking. When he was eleven, he was sent to live with his McNeil cousins for a year in a logging town near Fountain in Monroe County. The McNeils lived in a converted boxcar in the Pool Company lumber camp. Everyone who lived there worked for the same company and enjoyed the regular Saturday night dances at the camp. The hillbilly bands and fun stirred his enthusiasm for becoming a musician, but Daddy also liked the excitement of raiding the hidden stash of booze with the other boys. He discovered that a couple of beers or a few swigs from a bootleg jug could transform him from a quiet, insecure boy into a clever and confident young man.

In the summer of 1937, Mrs. Stone moved her family to Montgomery, the capital of Alabama, and immediately opened a boardinghouse at 114 S. Perry Street. Within a few years, she relocated to 236 Catoma Street, about a half block from the Jefferson Davis Hotel, the broadcasting source of WSFA radio.

By the time he reached Montgomery, Daddy was already set on having a career in music. In December of 1937 or 1938, wearing boots and a cowboy hat, and carrying a new Gibson Sunburst guitar, he entered an amateur talent contest at the Empire Theater in Montgomery. He won first prize with his original song, "WPA Blues," a parody of an old Riley Puckett recording, "Dissatisfied."

A lot of what I've learned about Daddy's first days as a musician has come from a man named Braxton (Brack) Schuffert. He was a young hillbilly singer who drove a truck for the Hormel Meat Packing Company and made regular stops at

Mrs. Stone's boardinghouse. He was already singing off and on over WSFA radio, and when Daddy found out about it, he started riding the Hormel truck with Brack, and they'd sing all day long.

Brack helped Daddy put together his first band, called Hank and Hezzy and the Drifting Cowboys, that Daddy told Mother about when they met. Brack thinks that Daddy might have started using the name *Hank* because of Hank Penny, a western swing band leader/singer in Birmingham who was popular at the time. Smith "Hezzy" Adair, the bass fiddler and a natural clown, Freddie Beech, a fiddler, and Daddy's sister Irene on vocals made up the little group. Nicknamed "Two-gun-Pete" by his neighbors in Georgiana, Daddy had been in love with the cowboy image since he was a child. He chose the name the Drifting Cowboys for his first band, and it would remain the same throughout his career.

In Brack's old '35 V-8 Ford, he and Daddy drove down to McKenzie, Georgiana, and Pigeon Creek, Alabama, to book Daddy's first shows at the schoolhouses there. At that time, there were many small schools scattered throughout the area, and, because each school was responsible for raising its own money, every one of them had a stage. The schools would bring all the people in on buses for thirty percent of the gate and the musicians would split the remaining seventy percent.

Then Daddy and Brack headed up to Greenville to book the Ritz Theater there. This is how Daddy's first tour was lined up.

In the late 1930s, Daddy traveled down to the Florida panhandle, where he met "Pappy" Neal McCormick and played in his band called the "Barn Dance Troubadours." The McCormicks treated Daddy like part of the family, and he sought out Pappy McCormick during many troubled times of his life.

When Daddy brought one of the Troubadours named Boots Harris, a steel guitar player, up to Montgomery and re-organized the Drifting Cowboys, his music began to take on a more professional sound. In February 1941 Hank Williams and his Drifting Cowboys made their radio debut on the new Montgomery station WCOV. One week later, they moved over to the more powerful station, WSFA. Singing mostly Roy Acuff tunes and other popular songs of the day, Daddy now

had the opportunity to introduce some of his original compositions to his new radio audiences.

Live music was the band's bread and butter, however. They
played at the Montgomery Armory on Madison Avenue,
where they started a regular Saturday night dance. On
Wednesday and Friday nights the band played square dances
at the Oak Park Pavillion, a big, round wooden building that
would hold one hundred couples. (One of Daddy's early band
members, M. C. Jarrett, swears that "there ain't nobody in the
world could call a square dance like Hank Williams, nobody!")
They continued to get bookings on the Ritz Theatre circuit and
also worked for awhile at the Cavalier Club, a big dance hall on
the Mobile Highway.

When they worked at the Cavalier Club, a character named
Juan Lobo, or Jack Wolf, who had been in the movies with
cowboy star Ken Maynard, sometimes joined them. Lobo
could take two lariats, spin them and jump through one, then
the other. He could also pop his sixteen-foot bullwhip and kill a
fly at any distance. He always drew quite a crowd whenever he
was there.

The Drifting Cowboys played in the established music spots,
like the American Legion Hall, but also in any place that would
have them, such as the room over Blackman's drugstore and
another one over the National Shirt store at the corner of Dex-
ter and Coach Streets. In between Georgiana and Chapman
was one of their favorite places to play, Thigpen's Log Cabin, a
dance hall where people brought their families on Saturday
nights.

Brack told me about one weekend at Thigpen's when Daddy
was short a steel guitar player and talked to a boy he knew
down there about helping him out. "I need a steel guitar man in
my band," he said, "and I want to hire you."

The boy told him, "Well, I just can play three chords."

Daddy answered, "You're the very man I want, I already got
a three chord fiddle player."

People who knew Daddy in those early days have told me he
looked like he was always thinking, always in a dream. He
wanted to write songs even then, music was just all that interested him. He didn't have a style of his own yet, and he would

just sing Roy Acuff and Ernest Tubb songs, and I'm told that even when he was only sixteen years old, he had a voice just as clear and strong as a grown man's.

Daddy and his band soon became well-known entertainers throughout southern Alabama on what was called the "blood bucket" circuit. His mother and Irene handled the bookings and collected the money at the door, usually charging twenty-five cents admission. Mrs. Stone also helped out when the crowds got rough, and they often did. Years later, Daddy still claimed, "There ain't nobody in the world I'd rather have alongside me in a fight than my mama with a broken bottle in her hand."

Daddy's mother did a lot to build his musical career. She boarded and fed his band members at her roominghouse, promoted and managed the shows, collected the money at the door and definitely was the dominant partner in the arrangement. I think Daddy loved his mother and was a little afraid of her at the same time. She'd fight back to back with her son in a brawl, but she didn't tolerate Daddy's drinking. When she tried to tell him what he could and couldn't do, it led to many arguments between them, sometimes even physical ones. In order to compensate for Daddy's frustrating behavior, Mrs. Stone became more and more domineering over him and he resented that, like any normal teenager would.

In August of 1942, Daddy and WSFA temporarily parted ways, probably due to his drinking habits. Seeking to escape Montgomery, he dropped out of school, which he had not attended regularly anyway. Then he signed up to work at the Kaiser Shipbuilding Corporation far out west in Portland, Oregon.

A musician friend named M. C. (Millard) Jarrett was with Daddy on that trip. "I met up with him in Chicago changing trains," recalls Jarrett. "It took maybe five or six days to get out there. Then Hank went to school about two days, but his eyes were so bad he couldn't make it. It was a good deal there. They paid you, and you had a place to stay and a dining hall where you could eat three meals a day and drink beer. We'd play and sing for loose change from the shipyard workers sitting out on the grass. I think Hank stayed out there about two weeks — he mostly stayed in the honky-tonks — then he called his mama and said, 'I need some money; I'm coming home.' Hank just wasn't born to do work like that."

He was completely broke when his mother wired him just enough money for train fare home. The trip lasted five days, and during that time he bummed one cigarette from a soldier but didn't have a thing to eat. His first cousin, Marie McNeil Harvell, was living and working at the boardinghouse at the time. She was pregnant and was sitting in an old rocking chair in the hallway when Daddy arrived home. "I can see him now," she says. "He asked, 'Gal, that baby hasn't come yet?' and I said, 'No, I was just waiting for you to come home.' He was near dead, he was starving. I went in there and set down at the kitchen table and I fed him myself. He was shaking so he couldn't get a fork in his mouth."

Before he went to the west coast, Daddy had been dating a girl named Kitty, but they broke up when he left town. It never would have been a strong enough relationship anyway to survive the powerful passion that Daddy felt from the first time he laid eyes on Audrey Mae Sheppard Guy.

❉ ❉ ❉ ❉ ❉

Hey, good-lookin', what-cha got cookin',
How's about cookin' somethin' up with me.

❉ ❉ ❉ ❉ ❉

The attraction between Daddy and Mother was mutual. Aunt Loretta used to tag along when Mother drove to neighboring towns to see Daddy playing with the medicine show. Sometimes, Mother had to make elaborate arrangements to get out of the house.

"Hank had a big Buick then and she had an Oldsmobile," says M. C. Jarrett, "The way it worked, they'd let me out a half-mile down and I'd walk by and whistle, that was the signal. By the time I got a quarter mile on the other side of the house, Audrey'd done be slipped off and met him already."

"Hank wasn't very well-loved at first by Audrey's daddy," Jarrett adds, "because for one thing she was still married. You couldn't get a divorce from a serviceman when he was overseas. That was the law during the war."

By the end of the medicine show circuit in and around Pike

County, however, no obstacle seemed too great for their love, and all of Daddy and Mother's plans for the future had been rearranged to include each other.

⸙ ⸙ ⸙ ⸙ ⸙

If you're meant for me like I'm meant for you,
Baby, we fit like a glove.
If you're lovin' me like I'm lovin' you,
Baby, we're really in love.

⸙ ⸙ ⸙ ⸙ ⸙

In early 1944, before they married, Mother and Daddy spent a short time working "side by side" welding ship parts with a blowtorch in the shipyards of Mobile, Alabama. "In the evenings," Mother remembered, "we'd go back to this terrible, little old hotel room and I'd wash out our clothes for the next day. Finally, one day I told him, 'This is just not it, Hank. I want to go back to Montgomery. I want to get a band together for you and get you back on a radio station and start working shows.' And that's exactly what I did."

Marie Harvell recalls that Daddy introduced Mother as his "secretary" the first time he brought her to Montgomery. "She came a lot after they started seeing each other," Marie says. "They'd stay at the boardinghouse, her and Lycrecia. They had a room next to mine, and Hank had the room next to them. That was the craziest house you ever lived in in your life. We played Rook — Hank and Audrey and myself and my husband — and Audrey helped out with answering Hank's fan mail. She began taking part in the business not too long after they started going together."

Don Helms, the steel guitar player who worked on and off with Daddy since 1943, remembers that Mother did some cooking for the band and collected admissions at the door when they played outside of Montgomery not long after she and Daddy met.

"There was an old farmhouse way out in the country by the river where we could go and relax for two or three days," he recalls. "Some of the guys would hunt and fish. Audrey would fry up the fish they caught, and the band would go into town at night and play and Hank would put her on the door."

Life on the road with Daddy and his band was just the sort of excitement mother craved, and the peaceful, loving Sheppard family offered the kind of stability that appealed to Daddy. Granddaddy was uncertain at first about the drinking, but Daddy's lovable, boyish ways soon won everybody's hearts. He liked to play and sing at family get-togethers and was known to stop by with his whole band to entertain a houseful of aunts, uncles, and cousins. Roy Acuff's "Great Speckled Bird" was a favorite of his, and Lynette remembers he played it for them a lot. And everybody remembers how quickly he grew attached to Mother's sweet, shy, two-year-old daughter — me.

One of Mother's girlhood friends will never forget one particular double date with Mother and Daddy. "We all went to a square dance at someone's house and a band was there, but Hank and Audrey took over. Everyone really enjoyed that. Audrey did not live far from there, so we carried her home first. On the way back to my house, we had a flat tire. We all got out, and I have never seen anyone change a flat tire as fast as Hank did. I told Audrey the next time I saw her about the flat tire and how fast he changed it. She said, 'I know, he can do anything with those fingers and that voice of his.' She told me that she was going to marry him. I wished them a lot of luck and she said, 'We will need it.' I did not know what she meant then, but I do now."

❁ ❁ ❁ ❁ ❁

My folks think I've gone crazy,
And I don't feel too sure.
And yet there's nothing wrong with me
That wedding bells can't cure.

❁ ❁ ❁ ❁ ❁

Daddy never stopped trying to get Mother to marry him. "Bless his heart," Mother said later, "but I was afraid. I was very hesitant because I knew he had this drinking problem, and I had never been around anybody who drank like that. We were living out of a trailer in Andalusia about a year after we met, and he was playing a club there. I had never been much of a cook, but I was trying to cook for the band and was taking up admissions at night. One afternoon, it was the fifteenth of De-

20127824

cember 1944, all of a sudden when he asked me I said, 'Yes.' He had been doing real good. He wasn't drinking, and I was real proud of him. So we took a couple of boys in the band and went over to see the justice of the peace who ran a filling station and got married."

CHAPTER 3

A License to Fight

By the time Daddy and Mother married, my grandfather, Shelton Sheppard, had torn down the old family homeplace and was building a new, more modern blockhouse, fully wired for electricity and complete with indoor plumbing. He had put up a temporary, wood two-room house next to the construction site for us to live in so we wouldn't have to live with relatives up the road. Mother packed up all her clothes and things and took up residence with Daddy in his mother's boardinghouse in Montgomery.

Lynette and I slept together in one bed in the little wood house, and she remembers that Daddy would come to see me right after he and Mother married. He'd come late at night, by himself when he was on the road. She says he would come to my side of the bed and stroke my hair and tell me how pretty I was. Sometimes he'd sing "You Are My Sunshine" and tell me I really was his sunshine. If I was asleep, he'd wake me up and sit and talk and sing for an hour.

She remembers that he came a number of times, but only one time that he had been drinking. The rest of the times he didn't seem to be intoxicated.

Daddy soon found himself in the middle of a struggle between his mother and his new wife. Both of them wanted to keep Daddy sober and to promote his singing career, but Mrs. Stone was not yet ready to turn Daddy over to another woman, and Mother was not willing to stand in the background. Daddy's solution was to get drunk, and the endless cycles of fights and reconciliations became more of a pattern in their lives.

"Aunt Lillie and Audrey didn't get along," says Daddy's cousin Marie. "I walked in the door one day and I heard this awful noise and I went in the bedroom. Aunt Lillie and Irene had Audrey down on the bed and they were fighting. I went to pull them off her, but my hand got tangled in Audrey's long hair. They ganged up on her quite often if I was there. But Audrey wasn't afraid of nobody. Hank knew how they did her, but what could he do about it? They had to stay because he wasn't making enough money to get out."

✿ ✿ ✿ ✿ ✿

If the wife and I start fussin' brother, that's our right,
'Cause me and that sweet woman's got a license to fight.

✿ ✿ ✿ ✿ ✿

Don Helms never saw Daddy and Mother argue right in front of him, but he heard them in other parts of the boardinghouse. "I would venture to say that no couple was ever more in love than Hank and Audrey," he recalled, "but when Hank would drink, she would raise hell and he'd raise hell because she raised hell. He would get to drinking more because she raised hell, and she raised hell because he was drinking more. That was a bad scene for everybody, but I think she was raising hell for all of us, really. When Hank was off of it [alcohol], he was just a regular kind of guy and they got along good."

M. C. Jarrett could also see how those early fights were tied to Daddy's drinking. "Hank and Audrey didn't fight when he wasn't drinking, but he never was hardly not drinking because he was so shy he needed that drink to bolster him up. She tried to keep him from drinking, though, and they were real lovey-dovey a lot of the time."

The arguments would bring Mother home frequently. They'd have a big fight, most of the time over Daddy's drinking. She'd come home, and before long he'd come and get her. Lynette recalls that Granddaddy took the side of the one who got there first. "If Audrey got there first and told Daddy her story, he took her side. If Hank got there first, he took his. I don't know why they didn't go somewhere else because Daddy was pretty much like Audrey, but they didn't."

❀   ❀   ❀   ❀   ❀

> Every time that you get mad,
> You pack your rags and go back to Dad.
> You tell him lies he don't believe,
> You're gonna change or I'm gonna leave.

❀   ❀   ❀   ❀   ❀

I think Daddy needed a father, and Granddaddy needed a son, and the two became very close. Daddy was as happy fishing on Buckhorn Creek or quail hunting in the woods beyond the farm with his father-in-law as he was doing anything anywhere else.

During early 1945 Daddy self-published two small songbooks containing the lyrics to many of the personal, sentimental, and spiritual songs he had written. The introduction to the second songbook described Daddy as "a long, lean, lanky fellow . . . He has brown eyes and black hair and a lazy good-natured air about him which endears him to his radio audience and to all who see him and his gang on their personal appearances throughout the South." That sounds like Mother describing Daddy to me, and I wonder how much she had to do with getting those books published.

She did say later that "the good and the bad—both financially and in love" was captured in the words to the songs in those songbooks. "We were separated several times in the early years of our marriage," she admitted. "Show life is hard when one is trying to get a start. Nights without sleep, days of drudgery, and short tempers don't promote better marriage relationships." She always went back, though, because she believed that "the heart of Hank Williams was great."

❀   ❀   ❀   ❀   ❀

> My darling, you left me and went away,
> You know my dear that I begged you to stay.
> But you said we were through dear, that was the end,
> But remember I told you you'd love me again.

❀   ❀   ❀   ❀   ❀

Mother had drive; she had ambition. That was her problem. She knew Daddy had the potential to really hit it big, to set the world on fire. She wanted to see him do those things, and when he let it drag on, she'd get impatient with him.

Mother was a very intelligent woman, and she was the backbone of Daddy. She was the one who had the good business sense, and Daddy was the one with the talent. I think she saw his talent when she fell in love with him, and from then on she was the one who got in touch with the right people or tried to maneuver him in their direction.

I'm not taking anything away from Daddy because Mother couldn't have done anything if he hadn't had the talent. I think Daddy was a genius. He was way ahead of his time. He just loved to entertain. He was content to write his feelings down in songs and sing them over the radio and to live audiences in and around Montgomery.

Mother wanted him to get further than staying in Montgomery and working the honky-tonks. She also hoped to make enough money to move out of the rowdy boardinghouse and into a place where she could bring me to live with them.

A woman named Bernice Turner described life in that boardinghouse for me. She and her husband Doyle came up to Montgomery from Panama City, Florida, late in 1945 to play with Daddy and the Drifting Cowboys. Daddy was well-known in the Florida panhandle because of his association with "Pappy" Neal McCormick and also because WSFA radio in Montgomery was strong enough to reach as far as Georgia, Mississippi, and Florida. So Bernice and Doyle were already acquainted with Daddy's talent and his reputation for heavy drinking when they accepted the job and moved into Mrs. Stone's boardinghouse.

Bernice remembers that the food was good and the boardinghouse was full of drunks. A day usually started with everybody sitting down to breakfast at a big table, maybe twenty feet long. Later they carried their instruments down to the Jefferson Davis Hotel for the live radio show that was making Daddy so popular throughout the South.

By the time they finished their broadcast and returned to the boardinghouse around noon, half the people there would be sitting around the radio drinking and crying — often from Daddy's singing and narration. Bernice says that even she and Doyle would be crying while they were humming harmony behind Daddy as he sang their favorite hymn, "Where Could I Go but to the Lord?"

The drinking at the boardinghouse got more serious in the afternoons, and the Turners went to a lot of movies to get away from it. Bernice has some very clear memories of the days when Daddy was one of the drunks:

> Hank was real tall and skinny and you would not think he could fight to look at him, but the man could fight a circle saw. I remember one particular time we were walking home from a movie and as we came in sight of the roominghouse, we saw Hank standing outside with a piece of a rocker in his hand that he had broken off. A guy named Blackie, a fiddle player, had a Coca-Cola bottle in his hand, and he was about half a block away. Hank was standing right in front of the house with no shoes on, reeling back and forth with that rocker piece in his hand. I have no idea what that fight was over.
>
> Blackie saw us and yelled, "Doyle, come and do something with Hank!" We just turned around and went back around the corner into another movie. I thought, *Let them kill each other if they want to.*

These incidents did not happen every day, I am told. Daddy would go for two or three weeks without drinking, and everything would be great. Mother and he were so much in love, Daddy would call her "Honey" and always had his arm around her. Everyone who knew them say it was obvious that he loved her, and they never had a cross word when he was sober.

Bernice says that although Daddy was the sweetest person in the world when he was sober, when he would drink, all the good times and laughter would end.

> The sober part was great, but when Hank would get drunk, he would jump onto Audrey or he'd run her off. He was very violent when he got drunk. After working in the field of alcoholism I think the reason he was being violent was that he was really saying, "Goddammit, leave me alone and let me drink. Let me drink all I want to drink."
>
> If Hank took one drink, he just would not stop until he didn't know he was in the world. That's how most alcoholics do. They

might drink one today or drink another one tomorrow and fool themselves with, "Well, I'm going to prove to myself that I can drink," but they don't. They keep going because this sets off a chemical reaction in the body until they crave more and more.

If somebody doesn't do something to give them an excuse for drinking, they'll make one up. Everybody plays their roles in helping the alcoholic survive these things. Usually it's the wife. After one of his drinking bouts, Hank would be like a little puppy dog trying to make up. Audrey would fuss at him for a couple of days, and then everything would be all right. In later years, she got tired of hearing, "I'm sorry."

Some years after Hank died, I was in Montgomery by myself and went out and spent hours at Hank's grave. As I cried, I thought back on really how happy the four of us were at that time, except when he would get on these drunks.

I drove over to the VFW club and went in and got a drink. That was one of Hank's favorite hangouts in Montgomery. You could get drinks there when you couldn't get them anywhere else. I remembered driving around in the car trying to find him when an important gig would be coming up. Audrey would be crying as we went to all the places we thought he might be. The smaller places, like down in Andalusia where he had played so long, hardly anyone would ask where he was if he wasn't there. They had gotten so used to it. But when we played larger places and shows where there was a lot of money involved, then all of us would start looking for him to get him sober.

At that time Daddy paid the Turners fifty-seven dollars a week in addition to their room and board, but he worked them seven nights a week. On Sundays they played at a club on the Mobile Highway right out of Montgomery. It was a classy place but could on occasion get pretty rough, like the time people started shooting from one end of the room to the other and the band had to hide behind the piano until it was safe enough to dash out the front door.

Bernice's husband had taught her to play a hard, off-beat rhythm guitar. With so much playing, she developed callouses on her fingers and when her husband would yell at her to play harder, she'd get mad and break strings from coming down too hard. One day she broke one at this same club, and Daddy turned to her and said, "Bernice, I'd rather have you on guitar than anybody I've ever had, but damn, you keep me broke buying guitar strings!"

Another regular night stand for Daddy and the Drifting Cowboys during those days was at a big roller rink, the Riverside Palladium, outside Andalusia. People flocked to hear Daddy there, but one night he had already gotten drunk and passed out in the hotel. Mother got somebody they knew to work at the door so she could play bass (Bernice says Mother "played stand-up bass as good as anybody did back then"), and she and the Turners played to a packed house. When people asked where Hank was, they just said he was sick. According to Bernice, it was hard then to find musicians you could keep sober.

Bernice also says that it was during some of these episodes that people would ask Mother why she didn't drink with Daddy to let him know how it felt. One night she did get drunk, but he was so drunk himself he couldn't have cared less. Mother started having "some sort of spell," and they had to take her to the hospital. "Believe me," says Bernice, "she almost died that night. She was sick for two or three days and just kept passing out. That is the only time I saw the girl drinking the whole time we were with them."

Another part of life in that boardinghouse that I have learned a lot about is the jealousy between Mother and Mrs. Stone. Daddy especially didn't like the way his mother and his wife tried to beat each other to his pocketbook when he got drunk. The truth of it was, though, that if they hadn't, he wouldn't have had a dime of it left.

It was either Mother or Mrs. Stone who would work the door when the band was playing for a live audience. Mother knew that if she didn't get the money, it would be gone because people would get around Daddy and get him drinking and he'd end up paying for the parties and booze. But Mrs. Stone was giving the band a place to stay and feeding them well. So, as Bernice says, "If Lillie could get the money, she kept it herself."

This was the kind of life Mother and Daddy had during the first years of their marriage — periods of drinking, fighting, separations, making up, and playing music every night!

By all accounts, Mother is the one who instigated the next change in their lives. It started with the trip to Nashville to pitch Daddy's songs to Fred Rose in September 1946. Mr. Rose, who wrote "Red Hot Mama," "'Deed I Do," and "Blue Eyes Crying in the Rain" among many others, had teamed up with "Grand Ole Opry" star Roy Acuff to form the first music publishing house expressly for hillbilly songs and writers.

The story of Fred Rose telling Daddy to sit down and write a song at that September meeting to prove his abilities as a songwriter was first mentioned by Daddy himself and has persisted as part of the Hank Williams legend. Here is Mother's version of what happened on that trip from a 1973 interview:

> I brought Hank to Nashville. I had heard about Fred Rose and Hank had written a few songs and I thought they were good, but who was I? I was so young at the time. I can't recall the date, but I know it was at one in the afternoon when Hank and I came from Montgomery on the train into Nashville and called Fred Rose. The nearer the time came to meet with Fred, the more nervous Hank got, and I said, "You're going if I have to push you every step of the way!" And I just about did, too.

> We met Fred at WSM at one of the small studios there. At that time, Fred took three or four of Hank's songs for different artists to do. But he said to Hank, "Boy, how do I know you wrote these songs? You might have bought them off of somebody. So," he said, "to prove to me that you can write, I'm going to give you a title, and I want you to take it back to Montgomery with you and write this song."

> So we go back to Montgomery with this title, "Mansion On The Hill." Somehow or other, Hank worked with this song and worked with it, but he never could do too much with it. I think the reason he couldn't was because it wasn't his idea. I think he was such a genius that to take someone else's idea and try to fit it in the way they wanted was a little bit rough for him.

> We were living in an apartment at the time in Montgomery, and one night I had just finished with the dinner dishes and I had sat down at the table in the little kitchen area and I started . . . "Tonight, down here in the valley. . . ." I just was coming along with it. After I got through with it, I walked into the room there and said, "Hank, what do you think of this?" Well, he really liked it. So between my lyrics and Hank's lyrics and some of Fred's, that's how "Mansion On the Hill" came about. For a long time I

wouldn't let nobody know I had anything to do with it because I wanted it to be all Hank. I wasn't really a writer; maybe I wrote a few, but he was the one.

     ❖   ❖   ❖   ❖   ❖

Tonight down here in the valley,
I'm lonesome and oh how I feel.
As I sit here alone in my cabin,
I can see your mansion on the hill.

     ❖   ❖   ❖   ❖   ❖

Regardless of who wrote "Mansion on the Hill," Mother had managed a way out of the boardinghouse, and on to bigger things.

CHAPTER 4

The Way to Keep
a Woman Happy

In the summer of 1946, Mother and Daddy rented a small house in Montgomery at 409 Washington Avenue and brought me up from Banks to live with them. It was our first home as a family. This was just after they had gone to Nashville and met Fred Rose, and Daddy was beginning to make a little money as a singer and songwriter.

It took me a while to adjust to going to sleep in a strange house. If I cried to go home to my grandparents' house, Mother and Daddy would say, "O.K., we'll take you back home." They'd put me in the back seat of the car and drive me around until I was asleep. Then Daddy would carry me back into the house and put me to bed. After I woke up there several mornings, I got accustomed to it, but I did miss living down on the farm.

The people who lived next door to us on Washington Avenue had carrier pigeons in pens backed up against the fence in the yard. I was fascinated by the birds, and the son in the family would explain to me how they sent the birds off to carry messages and how they found their way back home again.

I had just turned five years old, and I remember the first day Mother took me to kindergarten in Montgomery. I really didn't want to go, so she stayed with me the whole time. We were out on the playground, and the teacher was trying to get me to play with the other children. I must have sassed her a little because

Mother spanked me right there. After I got used to kinder-garten, though, I liked it just fine. And I liked living with Mother and Daddy.

Mother and Daddy had a good year in 1946-47. Daddy was writing more and more songs and beginning to record them in Nashville. Things began to take off in November 1946, when Fred Rose sent Daddy a contract for two of his songs, "When God Comes To Gather His Jewels" and "Six More Miles To The Graveyard," that he planned to have recorded by singer Molly O'Day.

Daddy wrote back:

> Dear Mr. Rose:
> I have received my contract. Thanks very much. Here's hoping you can send me some good news.
> I have 3 or 4 more numbers I'd like to send you. I think maybe you can use them. And I have several of which I'd like to get copyrighted.
>
> Sincerely,
> Hank Williams

In December Mr. Rose suggested Daddy's name to Sterling Records because they wanted to record a hillbilly singer. On December eleventh in WSM radio's Studio D (Castle Studios) in Nashville, Daddy recorded four sides for Sterling backed by the Oklahoma Wranglers (later known as the Willis Brothers). These historic recordings, which Daddy had composed over the preced-ing few years, were: "Calling You," "Never Again (Will I Knock On Your Door)," "Wealth Won't Save Your Soul," and "When God Comes and Gathers His Jewels."

Daddy was paid eighty-two dollars and fifty cents for each of the two sessions he did for Sterling, that one in December and the second one on February 13, 1947. The second session selections, "I Don't Care (If Tomorrow Never Comes)," "My Love For You (Has Turned to Hate)," "Honky-Tonkin'," and "Pan American" were also all his original compositions.

By April 1947, he had his first recording session with MGM Records, and one of the songs cut that day, "Move It On Over," about a husband who's "in the doghouse," was soon to put Daddy on the brink of stardom. The session also included three other of Daddy's originals: "I Saw The Light," "(Last Night) I Heard You Crying In Your Sleep," and "Six More Miles To The Graveyard."

❀   ❀   ❀   ❀   ❀

> Come in last night at half past ten,
> That baby of mine wouldn't let me in,
> So move it on over, move it on over,
> Move over li'l dog, 'cause the big dog's movin' in.

❀   ❀   ❀   ❀   ❀

The summer after kindergarten, I had my tonsils out and had to spend the night in the hospital. Mother and Daddy stayed with me as long as the hospital would let them, and then they were back bright and early the next morning. They brought me some crayons and a coloring book and made sure I got all the ice cream I wanted.

When I got home after my operation, I remember running in from outside one day to tell Mother I had spit up some blood, and she reassured me I was O.K. While we were talking that day, she said, "Lycrecia, Honey, don't you think it'd be nice if you started calling Hank 'Daddy'?" I had always called him "Hank" because that's what everybody called him. She told me later that he had asked her, "Do you think she'll ever call me Daddy?" After I started, he never let me call him Hank again. I really don't think he ever looked at me and said, "She's not mine; she belongs to someone else." Daddy even told people that I was the spitting image of him.

I spent the rest of that summer on the farm with my grandparents. When I went back to Montgomery to start the first grade, Daddy and Mother had bought a little brick house on Stewart Street out in a new subdivision. It had an awning in the front and a small step up to the porch. Daddy used to push me around on my tricycle in the front yard, and he liked to carry me on his shoulders. When his sister Irene and her husband J.T. would bring their two children to visit, Daddy played with all of us. He really loved kids, and he picked at us or teased us all the time.

Mother's youngest sister, Lynette, spent quite a bit of time visiting us in Montgomery. Daddy looked on her as another daughter to guide and care for. He was the one who decided it was time for her first haircut, when she was in the fourth or fifth grade. He was also responsible for recognizing that she needed glasses.

"I won't ever forget it," Lynette says. "We were sitting in the kitchen. We had had our supper and were still at the table. I was fooling with one of my eyes and he kept looking at me. Finally, he told Mother maybe she should take me to have my eyes examined. Sure enough, I needed glasses. He was very observant."

It was mostly in the summers or on weekends that I went on the road with them. I remember loading up the car and sitting on the lap of the bass fiddle player, Lum York. The band played at schoolhouses and theaters and places like that, and Lum always did a comedy thing. At some point, he'd paint black dots on his face, put on baggy pants, and do a skit while he played the bass. Sometimes I got so tired before the show was over that I'd lie down in Lum's bass fiddle case and go to sleep until they were ready to go home.

I have talked to Lum a lot about this period when I started to be around Mother and Daddy more. He knew Daddy pretty well at that time, and he remembers a lot of good things. He says Daddy didn't like to hear a person criticized just because he was handicapped or down on his luck.

"We'd be ridin' around and he'd see a black guy playin' a guitar and singin' and he'd always stop and pick him up and ride him around and let him play for us for a couple of hours and then he'd give him some money when he let him out. Anybody playin' on the street like that he'd usually give them a little money."

                ❀   ❀   ❀   ❀   ❀

> So help your brother along the road,
> No matter where you start.
> For the God that made you made them, too,
> These men with broken hearts.

                ❀   ❀   ❀   ❀   ❀

Lum also mentioned how Daddy always closed the shows out with hymns. "Just about every show Hank did on the stage or radio he ended that way, and he didn't want nobody to cut up or hardly move while he did them. He wanted respect for the sacred numbers when he sang them or when anybody else sang them."

I remember how much Daddy liked to read romance comics, and so does Lum. "He used to want me to come over to his place with him. I'd say I didn't want to go, but he'd keep at me. Then as soon as I'd ride over there, he'd pick up a book, one of those comic books, and sit there and read. I'd get up and say, 'I'll see you directly.' Two hours later he'd be back over my house sayin', 'Come on over!' I'd say, 'Hank, you're not going to do nothin' but sit there and read!'"

Lynette also remembers that Daddy read a lot. "Hank was a very smart man. I've come across so many people that thought he was illiterate. Well, he was not. He constantly had a book in his hand. He read poetry, he read comic books — the floorboard of the car was always full of comic books. If he was stretched out on the sofa, he would either be reading the paper or a book or something."

Lum told me that "Once we went to a picture show, just me and Hank, and this cowboy in the movie had turned this girl over his lap and was spanking her. Hank turned to me and said, 'That's what you got to do to these women,' and later on that's what he done to Audrey."

That might have happened just before an incident that I remember. We had all piled into this old car of Daddy's to head out to a show, and we were waiting for Mother and Daddy but they didn't come out. I was sitting on Lum's lap, and once or twice I started to get down and go see where they were, but Lum talked me out of it. Finally, I went back in the house to see what was holding them up. They had gotten into an argument of some kind, and Daddy had Mother down across his lap, whipping her like a little kid. I guess he must have already swatted her about one time, and as he came down the second time he looked up and saw me. He stopped right there and let her up. They didn't say anything, not a word. We all went out and got in the car and went to the show. I guess Mother had made him mad about something, and he decided she needed to be whipped.

❄   ❄   ❄   ❄   ❄

"The way to keep a woman happy
And make her do what's right,
Is love her in the morning,
Bawl her out at night."

❄   ❄   ❄   ❄   ❄

Lynette says that Daddy and Mother always tried to control their tempers and arguing around their children, including her. She doesn't recall much unhappiness during her visits with us in Montgomery, but she does know that on at least one occasion while they were still living there, Mother insisted Daddy take treatment for alcoholism. The family was talking about how bad he was drinking, and Mother told him she would not live with him unless he went to a hospital.

Daddy went to the hospital a lot of times to get sobered up. Lum remembers having to take him over to Prattville, about twelve miles away, where the nurses didn't know him too well. There in Montgomery just about everybody knew him, and they'd give him whiskey. "He was good at sneakin' a fast drink, too," says Lum. "A couple of steps or so out of the boardinghouse, you'd come right in the door of a little cafe. I've toted many a bottle of beer under my arm back to the house. He'd meet me in the bathroom and drink that beer down so quick you wouldn't hardly know it.

"One time he told me to come over there and he said, 'I done learned how to drink.'

"I said, 'Hank, I been learnin' that for years.'

"He said, 'No, I'm not talking about that. I can drink and I can quit when I want to.'

"I said, 'Hank, that's fine, I'm glad to hear that.'

"He said, 'Come on.'

"I said, 'Uh oh.'

"So we got in the car and drove around the corner, and after we'd stopped in the first beer joint I said, "Uh oh" again. That's where I left him. The next morning I found out he had gotten drunk and hit two cars. I walked in and Hank was layin' in bed, and I said, 'Yeah, I see you done learned how to drink, uh huh.'

"He said, 'I don't want to hear nothin' about it.'

Like anyone who spent much time around Daddy and Mother, Lum was aware of their up-and-down relationship. From what he says, little things could set them off. "Sometimes Hank and Audrey would be singin' and she'd break time and Hank would get onto her and she'd get mad, and the first thing you know they'd be separated for two or three days. Then he'd go and get her, and everything would go good for a while. Then she might go downtown to buy a pair of shoes, but he'd think she gave too much money for them and they'd have a little fuss about that."

And Lum remembers one time Mother had left Daddy and had taken me to stay in a hotel. Daddy had Lum take money around to the desk clerk and tell him to give it to Mother so we could buy food. I don't remember that.

Daddy had three more sessions for MGM in 1947. On August fourth, he recorded "Fly Trouble," "Honky-Tonk Blues," "I'm Satisfied With You," and "On the Banks of the Old Pontchartrain." On November sixth and seventh, with the exception of one Fred Rose number, "Rootie Tootie," Daddy returned to recording his own material, with "I Can't Get You off of My Mind," "I'm a Long-Gone Daddy," "My Sweet Love Ain't Around," "The Blues Come Around," and "Mansion on the Hill."

On May 6 Daddy wrote to Fred Rose about his new radio program on WSFA at six in the morning. "If you have any records that you want plugged, send them to me," he offered. An August nineteenth letter to Mr. Rose mentions a duet of "I Saw the Light" that Daddy had recorded with Mother and sent up to Nashville along with "that thing — entitled 'Everything's OK.'"

A close, personal bond was developing between the two men. Fred Rose smoothed out some of the rough edges in Daddy's songs, and Daddy confided in Mr. Rose about the strains of constant battle with his beautiful, hot-tempered wife.

Daddy was working the road and we didn't have a lot of money, but there weren't too many things I wanted. I was raised with no money and didn't ask for very much. I just remember that we were a family, and we were happy. And I always got what I asked for at Christmastime.

For Christmas 1947, in the new house, I had asked for a doll and a dollbed. That's the only thing I wanted. On Christmas morning I didn't get a lot of toys, but I had that doll and doll-bed. The doll had a fancy white dress on, and the bed had a fancy white cover. I thought it was the most wonderful sight I had ever seen. I know it was extremely hard for Mother and Daddy to get those things for me back then.

Mother and Daddy's marital problems grew more serious as the year 1948 began. In February Mother took me back to my grandparents' farm and enrolled me in the Enon School to finish the first grade. In March Daddy sought refuge from his troubles in Pensacola, Florida, with his old friend Neal Mc-Cormick and his family.

I didn't like going to the Enon School, and I was scared to death of my teacher. I can remember getting off the bus one day and telling Mother that I had failed a spelling test. The teacher had told me and everyone else who failed that she was going to give that test again the next day, and anyone who failed that time would get a whipping.

I was terrified, so Mother said she'd help me learn the spell-ing words. I studied and studied that night. Mother asked me to spell the words, and I spelled every one of them right for her. She said, "O.K., Honey, you're going to do just fine." She gave me the spelling words again the next morning just before I got on the schoolbus, and I spelled them all. But when I got to school that day, I was so petrified that I failed the test again, and I got a whipping. I just dreaded going to that school every day. I was beginning to be very shy, especially in school.

April 1948 was a month of mixed blessings. On April 12 Daddy signed a three-year exclusive songwriting contract with Acuff-Rose that guaranteed him fifty dollars a month against future royalties and also promised to publish at least six of his songs a year. This accomplishment could not have softened the blow, however, when Mother filed for divorce on April 28, stat-ing in her complaint: "Hank Williams, my husband, is twenty-four years of age. He has a violent and ungovernable temper. He drinks a great deal, and during the last month he has been drunk most of the time. My nervous system has been upset, and I am afraid to live with him any longer."

By the time the divorce was granted in May, though, Mother

and Daddy had reconciled, and a June postcard Daddy sent to Fred Rose from Norfolk, Virginia, has a cartoon drawing of a lady riding a mule with the caption, "I'm not the first jackass to support a woman." The brief message on the back, "Having Big Time" and signed "Hank and Audrey," was his way of letting Mr. Rose know that things were back under control at home. Exactly one year later, their divorce was declared null and void.

❀   ❀   ❀   ❀   ❀

Like a hog a-rootin' up under a fence,
Like a flop-eared mule that ain't got no sense,
I've been a fool about you for away too long . . .

CHAPTER 5

Picking up Speed
on the Hayride

The "Louisiana Hayride" opened in Shreveport, Louisiana, in April 1948. It was a country music variety show broadcast over the 50,000 watt KWKH radio station, and Fred Rose saw the new barn dance as an opportunity to showcase Daddy's talents. The "Grand Ole Opry" in Nashville, Tennessee, Country Music's most important stage show, was Mr. Rose's ultimate goal for Daddy, but first they needed to prove to the Opry staff that Daddy was really up and coming and that his drinking problems were a thing of the past. So, during the late spring or early summer of 1948, Mother and Daddy made a trip to Shreveport to explore the possibilities there.

Directly across the street from the KWKH studio and offices was a row of shops, including a twenty-four-hour eatery called the Bantam Grill. It was the favorite hangout for the KWKH crowd to pass the time in between their appearances. That's where Daddy met Tillman Franks, a bass player and sometimes promoter for the "Louisiana Hayride" performers. Daddy did not want to move to Shreveport unless he knew he could get some work there. As a regular on the show, he would only make twenty-five dollars a week, or up to thirty-five after he got a sponsor. Tillman promised to help him out, and later on that trip Mother and Daddy were treated to a catfish dinner at the home of Tillman's parents.

I don't remember my first trip to Shreveport. Lum York says

I didn't go when the band first went in early August. "I got to their place in Montgomery about one in the morning," Lum recalls, "and they had everything all ready. We loaded up — I had my bass on the top of the car — and two guys from Florida come with us, Clyde Criswell and George Brown, a fiddle player and a guitar player. We arrived on a Sunday evening and stayed in a hotel in Shreveport not far from the radio station for three or four days. Then we all moved into an apartment at 4802 Mansfield, across from the railroad tracks. Later I moved to a hotel uptown."

Daddy's weekday radio show debuted on Wednesday, August 4, at 5:15 A.M. He made his first appearance on the "Louisiana Hayride" on Saturday night, August 7.

I do remember that we had a big time in Louisiana. I really enjoyed living there, the little time we stayed, and the people there appreciated Daddy's music. We made a lot of friends, and everyone treated us real nice; it was like one big family. The Bailes Brothers (Walter, Johnnie, and Homer) were the hottest act on the Hayride. Johnnie Wright and Jack Anglin (known together as Johnnie and Jack) and their Tennessee Mountain Boys with Miss Kitty Wells were also big attractions. Johnnie and Jack had left the "Grand Ole Opry" in Nashville to help open the Hayride. Kitty was later known as the Queen of Country Music, and she became a close friend to Mother. Other good friends of Mother and Daddy were Curley and Georgia Williams and Zeke and Helen Clements.

Everyone tried to get extra bookings during the week just to make a living. Tillman Franks made good on his promise to help Daddy and organized a number of shows at high school auditoriums in Texas, Alabama, and Arkansas. But sometimes the turnout was very poor, and after two or three months of making no money, Daddy had to disband the Drifting Cowboys.

Johnnie Wright, together with Johnnie Bailes, bought Daddy's old Chrysler and hired Kyle Bailes and Tillman Franks to go out and book their package show. It consisted of Johnnie and Jack and the Tennessee Mountain Boys featuring Miss Kitty Wells, the Bailes Brothers, and Hank Williams. They were successful, and those shows were where Daddy introduced his new audience to a tune popular with the folks back in Montgomery called the "Lovesick Blues."

Daddy was having a big time in Louisiana, too. Tillman Franks says, "It wasn't long before Hank got action. When he first sang 'Lovesick Blues' and wobbled his knees, he was home."

When I entered the second grade in Shreveport that September, I was very timid about getting up in front of the class and talking or answering questions. Every day I had to stay after school because I hadn't done my homework or I hadn't finished my classwork or something. Mother always had to pick me up because I missed the schoolbus.

One day when she picked me up she said, "Lycrecia, if you have to stay after school tomorrow, I'm going to whip you when you get home." Now Mother was not one who whipped a lot, but she didn't have to. When she said in an authoritative voice, "Lycrecia, don't do that again," I just didn't do it.

I had to stay after school the next day, and she had to pick me up. When we got home, she said, "O.K., come in here. I'm going to have to whip you." I dreaded it so much. She laid me across her knee and wore out my fanny. Well, I didn't have to stay after school anymore. I knew I didn't want any more whippings.

Johnnie and Jack were also songwriters for Acuff-Rose, and Mother and Daddy had first become acquainted with them through Fred Rose and Fred's son Wesley. Mr. Rose's eyesight was poor, so Wes would drive his father down to Shreveport regularly to see their writers. If they had any new material, they'd all go over to the radio station and put the songs on dubs, or demonstration disks, for Mr. Rose to take back with him to Nashville.

In late December 1948 Mother and Daddy left me with my grandparents in Alabama, dropped Kitty and Johnnie off in Nashville, and drove on to Cincinnati, Ohio, for Daddy's first recording session in more than a year. On the twenty-second, he recorded "Lost On the River," "I Heard My Mother Praying for Me," (both duets with Mother), "There'll Be No Teardrops Tonight," and "Lovesick Blues." Daddy did not write

"Lovesick Blues." It was copyrighted in 1922 by Irving Mills and Cliff Friend, two Tin Pan Alley songwriters.

Clyde Baum, a mandolin player in Johnnie and Jack's band, accompanied Mother and Daddy to Cincinnati for the session. He remembers that Fred Rose didn't want Daddy to record "Lovesick Blues." He thought there was nothing to it and it was a twenty-year-old "dog." Daddy insisted, and finally Mr. Rose agreed, with the condition that it wouldn't take up too much time.

"They had a microphone up close to the door of the studio for Hank to sing in," Clyde Baum recalls. "He was facing the band, which was lined up against the wall at the far end of the studio. Fred Rose was kind of at an angle to the left of him. Directly, Fred said, out of the blue sky, 'Well, O.K., record your song, Hank. If you musicians go through it the first time without making a mistake, you'll get time and a half.' Hank turned around to look at Fred and said, 'You're mighty damned free with my money!' just as the recording began. I don't know how they managed to get that comment off the record."

Daddy knew he had an audience waiting for that song because of what had been happening on the Hayride. Bob McNett, who was playing guitar for cowgirl singer Patsy Montana, remembers well the night he first heard Daddy sing "Lovesick Blues" on the stage of the "Louisiana Hayride."

"They simply would not let him off the stage. It impressed me that without any warning of any kind, suddenly Hank gets up and sings a song most of them hadn't heard before and gets a reaction that strong. The program director, Horace Logan, had a rough job that night trying to get the commercials on. He pleaded with the audience, but people wouldn't be still. Usually when an artist goes out to sing a song the audience has never heard before, they might show they like the song, but they won't tear the house down."

On January 9, 1949, the *Shreveport Times* ran an article entitled "'Lovesick Blues' About To Be Released" and stated, "Capacity crowds at the 'Louisiana Hayride' nearly 'tear the house down' for encores of 'Lovesick Blues.' This, among other reasons, necessitated the advance sale of tickets to the Saturday night KWKH songfest."

The next day, January 10, five months after Daddy's arrival

in Shreveport, the *Times* announced that the Shreveport Syrup Company was presenting a new Monday through Friday series at 8:15 A.M. starring Hank Williams, "one of America's top-ranked folk singers."

Daddy was soon working all day every day. He got over to the radio station extremely early five days a week for 5:15 A.M. and 6:30 A.M. segments before his 8:15 A.M. "Johnny Fair Syrup Show." Between shows he spent time at the Bantam Grill, which Daddy called "the beanery." Murrell Stansell, who owned and operated the Bantam, remembers that Daddy wasn't too sociable at that time of day and would sometimes sit for long periods on a stool at the counter just drinking coffee and not talking to anyone.

"He'd say to me, 'Give me a roll of nickels.' More than anything else," recalls Stansell, "he loved to play the marble machine, or gambling pinball machine. He'd be here playing my pinball table, and his band would have to pull him away to get him up to the studio on time."

Murrell Stansell also remembers how much Daddy loved catsup. He even poured it on his waffles that he ordered every morning for breakfast. "I wanted to stop selling him the waffles," he jokes. "I was only gettin' twenty cents for them, and he would use up a whole bottle of catsup that cost me eight or ten cents!"

Daddy may have been quiet at the Bantam, but he let loose when he got on the air. Lum York had gone to live on a farm in the country after the band broke up, and every day when Daddy's show was about to come on over KWKH, Lum would go into the house and turn on the radio. Then he'd get himself a biscuit and bore a hole in it, pour syrup into the hole, and eat it while he was listening to Daddy. When he told Daddy what he was doing, Daddy incorporated the story into his promotion for Johnny Fair Syrup. Then he'd say, "Man, that's real eatin'!" He called himself the "old syrup sopper" on the show and was soon selling enough syrup to bring the company out of serious financial trouble.

Tillman Franks describes Daddy as "so natural. He would give himself to the audience every time he hit the stage. He could tear an audience right up. He'd sing a sad song and make them cry and then sing kind of a silly song. I asked him one time how could he go out there and sing so hard and put so much into a song. He said, 'Tillman, I like to hear me sing, I don't care whether they like me or not. I just like to sing, and I give it what I've got. If they like it, well and good, but I don't worry none about it.'"

Johnnie Wright and his wife, Kitty Wells, spent a lot of time on the road with Daddy and believe they've never seen a better entertainer in all their years of performing. He seemed to know what people liked and was just plain down-to-earth and a lot of fun, on stage and off.

Johnnie remembers a time in Lake Charles, Louisiana. "Back then," he says, "we'd go into a town, and the radio station, which covered all the territory where we were playing, would give us a thirty-minute spot or so. The band would set up and play and plug the date for that night. Hank was there, the Bailes, Kitty, all of us, and we were doing this program. I was playing this character called Cousin Nimrod and plugging the shows for that night.

"Johnnie Bailes called Hank up to the mike and asked him, 'Hank, do you have anything you'd like to say?'"

"Hank answered, 'Yes, sir, I just want to say that I've had a lot of fun here today, and I'm going to have a hell of a lot more tonight!' Everyone started laughing because back in those days, no one was supposed to say words like *hell* over the air."

Mother was not having nearly as much fun in Louisiana as the rest of us. Within weeks after our move to Shreveport, she became pregnant and, while she and Daddy were excited with the news, she remained sick for the entire nine months she carried Hank, Jr. The Louisiana heat and humidity and the distance from her family in Alabama made it worse for her. She was extremely nervous. She couldn't be on her feet for very long, and she could hardly stand for her clothes to touch her. No matter what she did, she couldn't get comfortable. She was very edgy then, and I heard Mother and Daddy get into fusses several times in Louisiana. But most of the time, overall, we had a happy family life.

In addition, Mother had only been able to perform with Daddy for a short time in Shreveport before she outgrew her cowgirl outfits and felt too sick to do much traveling. So, as

Daddy's career began to blossom and started to keep him out on the road and away from home, she was left behind feeling unhappy and frustrated.

Because the Hayride performers were all so close though, Mother was able to form friendships with several of the other KWKH wives. Kitty was busy traveling the road with Johnnie and Jack during the week, but Helen Clements, wife of singer/songwriter/musician Zeke Clements, was good company for her. Sometimes after Mother sent me off to school, she and Helen would go on over to the Bantam Grill, drink a soda, and talk and wait for their husbands to come off the air. Then they would walk across the street to join them.

One time Mother and Daddy and I had been visiting Zeke and Helen over at their trailer. I had gone to the bathroom and seen this little bowl of bath oil beads, and they were so pretty. I just picked one up and put it in my pocket, like a kid'll do. On the way back home, I was sitting on the floorboard of the car playing with it. Mother looked back and asked me, "Lycrecia, where did you get that?" I said, "Over at Aunt Helen's." She said, "Did you ask her for it?" And I said, "No, ma'am, I didn't." She said, "That means you stole it, doesn't it?" and I said, "Well, yes, ma'am, I guess so."

When we got home, she told me to call Helen and apologize to her. I remember calling up and telling Helen I was sorry, and she was real nice and said it was O.K. Mother thought it was very important for me to learn I couldn't just take stuff, and she was right.

The winter we moved to Shreveport, I outgrew my winter coat. Momma and Daddy didn't have enough money to buy another one, so Mother called Helen and asked her if there was anything she could do with my old one. Helen told her that she could put some velvet on the sleeves to make them longer and around the bottom to give it enough length, and that's what she did. The coat lasted another winter.

On March 1–2, 1949, Daddy was back in Nashville in the Castle Studios again. Mother was with him, and they recorded two duets together, "Dear Brother" and "Jesus Remembered Me." Daddy finished up the sessions with "Lost Highway," "May You Never Be Alone," "Honky-Tonk Blues," "Mind Your

Own Business," "You're Gonna Change (Or I'm Gonna Leave)," and "My Son Calls Another Man Daddy."

When the *Shreveport Times* welcomed Daddy home on March 6, it noted that " 'Lovesick Blues' . . . ranks eleventh in this week's *Billboard* poll of 'Most Played Juke Box Folk Records.' This is a nationwide survey conducted by the amusement journal. In this section of the country it probably tops the list. The three record distribution centers which serve the KWKH listening area, New Orleans, Dallas, and Houston, report total sales of more than 35,000 copies of 'Lovesick Blues' in three weeks time."

Bob McNett had started playing guitar for Daddy after Patsy Montana's band broke up. He remembers the day Tillman Franks handed Daddy the copy of *Billboard* that showed "Lovesick Blues" had reached number one. "He laid the magazine down," Bob recalls, "and he sat there silent for hours and hours and I believe he was scared, really scared. He was overwhelmed. I think he felt like he was stepping into the unknown, and he was frightened but, at the same time, in the clouds a little bit. I've often thought that what went through his mind was, 'I am the same country boy that I was back in Montgomery, Alabama. I'm the guy who loves to sing and entertain and now they think I'm something else; they think I'm a big star. How will I measure up to what they think of me now when I am no different than I ever was.' He sat with no changed expression, looking straight ahead, like in a trance."

✿ ✿ ✿ ✿ ✿

I'm proud to be called countrified,
Makes me happy as can be,
And, friend, I'm here to tell you now
There'll be no change in me.

✿ ✿ ✿ ✿ ✿

McNett saw a lot of sides to Daddy in those early months of his rise to stardom. He saw Daddy's impish sense of humor and good-natured personality, and also how he was devoted to his family. "What impressed me most about Hank," he says, "is that he was honest and sincere on stage. He didn't add frills to his shows or put on any big fanfares. He just sang his songs from his heart and communicated those personal feelings directly to every member of the audience.

> Hank wasn't one to open up and come up and talk to you and tell you how much he thought of you. He didn't do that, but he'd give himself away sooner or later about how big his heart really was. Because he did care, he cared deeply about people. One time we were on the way back from either Alexandria or Monroe, Louisiana, and Hank was stretched out in the back of the car. He had been drinking lightly, but he was not drunk. All of a sudden he reached up over the back and got me around the neck and hugged me. I remember the feel of that unshaved face. He had never done anything like that before, and I was dumbfounded. And he said, "This is the best old so and so I ever knew," and then he laid back down. There was never anything like that before or after.
>
> Another time that made an impression on me was when Hank and one of the boys were fooling around in the back seat of the car. By accident, Hank's knee came up and hit Felton Pruett in the nose hard enough to black the guy's eye. Hank felt so terrible. He wanted to get to the doctor right away and have it taken care of. This was the first time I really saw how much he cared about other people. He was almost ready to cry because he had hurt that guy.

In mid-March 1949 Mother and Daddy signed the papers for a new house on lot 20 in the Modica Subdivision in Bossier City, just outside of Shreveport. Daddy also acquired a new, black Packard limousine about that time. He got it by taking over the payments from a man on the Hayride named Billy Byrd after Byrd's gospel quartet was forced to disband.

On April 3 the *Times* reported that Hank Williams had taken his first airplane ride when he returned to Nashville to record "Wedding Bells" and "I've Just Told Mama Good-bye" on March 20. That must have been about the time we moved into our new house. Advertisements for the Hayride appearing in the newspaper now placed Daddy's name first on the list of KWKH performers.

I got a new set of wheels, too. Soon after we moved, Mother and Daddy bought me a brand-new blue and white bicycle. I had learned to ride down on my grandparents' farm, and by now I had a friend that I played with all the time who had a bike. He was the nephew of Mrs. Scoggins, the woman who later came to work for us after the baby was born.

My friend and I spent every hour together when we weren't in school, exploring on our bicycles and fishing with bacon for crawfish in the river. I was a tomboy, so whatever he wanted to do was fine with me. We were always outside playing or building something.

There was a river or canal that ran down behind the houses. Some of the older kids had built a raft. They would get on it and push themselves across the river and back with long poles. Daddy had told me never to get on it by myself. I wanted to ride that raft so bad, but I was too shy to ask the other kids for a ride.

One day I was at the river by myself. Mother and Daddy were in the house, and I was fishing for crawfish. I decided just to ride the raft out to the middle of the river and back. I got on the raft and pushed out, but I never got to the middle because I got stuck. I couldn't get back to the shore, either. Finally I got scared enough to call for Daddy. It took a long time for him to hear me, but when he looked out and saw me, he came running.

I was never so glad to see anyone. He waded out and pulled the raft back to shore. I just knew he was really going to fuss at me, but he just hugged me and told me never to do it again. "I'll take you out on it if you want to go," he promised. He was a terrific father.

The Easter that we were in Louisiana, we went over to Caddo Lake, outside of Shreveport, for a picnic with Kitty and Johnnie and their kids, Bobby and Ruby, Johnnie Bailes and his family, and Jack and Louise Anglin. Mother was very pregnant with Hank, Jr. We painted Easter eggs and had an Easter egg hunt.

Mother had bought me a white, silky-looking dress with green or pink embroidery on it. I could hardly wait to wear that dress; I thought Easter was never going to come. I had white shoes and socks and a little white hat and gloves. Someone made a picture of Ruby Wright and me standing together, both wearing our little hats and dresses. We thought we were really something that day.

I do not remember the story that Johnnie Wright tells about that Easter Sunday in 1949:

We just went out to have a good time, to hide eggs and let the kids find them. We took a big tub of beer iced down. Nobody even knew that Hank had a problem with drinking then. But Audrey knew, and I think that's the reason she hadn't wanted to go, on account of the beer. But she finally agreed to go, and we all got out there and we started drinking beer and Hank started drinking beer, too. Of course, Audrey knew that when he took one he'd want another one. We didn't really drink too much out there that day, maybe four or five beers. The women were all drinking, too, except Audrey.

After the Easter egg hunt, we all went over to Johnnie Bailes' house. Audrey was getting pretty far along in her pregnancy, so she and Lycrecia went home. I think she was also kind of mad at Hank for drinking and cutting up. We all sat around at Johnnie's and sang a few songs.

That night when Hank went home, he and Audrey got into an argument. Audrey had taken an ice pick and punched holes in all of Hank's tires so he couldn't drive, and he was so mad he tore up some of the furniture in the house and throwed everything around. Audrey called Kitty and asked her to come over there. I went with her, and Hank was already in bed when we got there.

Audrey had some sleeping pills the doctor had given her, and she asked Kitty to get her one and they discovered they were all gone. Audrey said, "Well, he's taken those pills." But she didn't know how many he had taken, so she had to call the doctor to come over and check Hank out.

I was sleeping in the room with Hank at the time, laying over against the wall on the bed. The doctor shook Hank, and Hank raised up and looked at him and the doctor asked, "How many of them pills did you take?" Hank says, "You know too damn much" and flopped back down. So the doctor went out and told Audrey Hank was all right, not to worry about him.

That is the earliest recollection anybody has mentioned of Daddy's taking pills. He was pretty much on good behavior while he was in Shreveport and only went off the wagon two or three times that anyone can remember. As Tillman Franks said, "Hank couldn't handle success too good — success and his personal problems — he just couldn't handle them. And it was all happening so fast."

Bob McNett recalls one occasion when he saw Daddy drinking. "He did his show perfectly fine, and, I never will forget this, after the show he confided in me, 'I wish I could get away from signing autographs because people are going to smell the liquor on my breath.' I didn't have any sense of how severe his drinking could be, but obviously Audrey did."

Like a lot of people, Bob believes that Mother and Daddy basically loved each other very much. He remembers his first experience with any anxiety on Mother's part was early one morning after the band came home from a show. Mother called him at the station to ask if Daddy had been drinking because he hadn't gotten home yet, and she was apparently quite concerned.

"The remainder of the time in Shreveport, I don't recall being a witness to any more problems between them." Bob says. "I do have a strong memory, though, that Hank thought the world of Lycrecia and was really excited about the new baby coming."

Lynette and Grandmama came to visit late that spring to help Daddy with taking care of Mother. Lynette and I heard Mother and Daddy arguing over a name for the baby. Daddy hated the name Hiram and said he wouldn't put that on anybody, especially his own kid. Obviously, she gave in on that instance.

Lynette also remembers how big and uncomfortable Mother was and how Daddy knocked himself out trying to please her. He went out and bought a record player with a cabinet and a chair and hassock so she could sit and put her feet up and listen to music. She was not easy to please during those months.

I recall one time in particular when Mother and Daddy were fussing. Mother had been to the hospital several times to have the baby, but it had been false labor. What they were fussing about I don't know, but Mother was sitting on the couch and Daddy had brought her a glass of water. She had set it on the coffee table after she drank some of it.

Daddy was standing up, kind of pacing back and forth, when Lynette and I walked in from outside. We sat down on the other side of the couch and didn't say anything. Mother got

Above: Mother at about age three on Granddaddy's farm. *Right:* Mother (on the right) at about age thirteen, with her sister Loretta and brother Eldridge. *Below:* Mother, Great-grandmother Hardin, Grandmama (Artie Mae), and Granddaddy (Shelton) Sheppard. Loretta and Eldridge are standing in front.

Left: Daddy as a teenager standing in front of his mother's boardinghouse on Catoma Street. *Above:* Mother's high school picture. *Below left:* Mother at age eighteen.

Above: Daddy as a young man.
Right: The first picture of
Mother and Daddy taken after
their December 1944 wedding.
[Courtesy of Delila Ellis]

Above: Hank Williams and the Drifting Cowboys, around 1946.
That's Bernice and Doyle Turner on the left side of the picture and
Mother and Daddy on the right. [Courtesy of Bernice Turner]
Below: An earlier version of Hank Williams and the Drifting
Cowboys. Standing (left to right) are Winston (Red) Todd, Daddy,
Joe Pennington, and Sonny Norrell. That's Lum York in front,
clowning as usual. [Courtesy of Lum York]

Right: Daddy and me posed in front of his old Chevrolet. Notice Mother's shadow in the foreground. *Below:* Daddy and me with some of the hogs he had bought for Granddaddy's farm.

Above left: Mother and me in front of Mrs. Stone's boardinghouse during our Montgomery days. *Above:* Mother and me on a block wall at the house of Grandmama and Granddaddy's farm. *Left:* Me later in front of Mother and Daddy's car in Shreveport.

Right: Mother with Daddy's first cousin, Marie. *Below:* Mother, Daddy's mother Lillie Stone, and me in front of our home on Stewart Street in Montgomery.

Left: Mother and Daddy had their bad times. *Below:* They had their good times as well. [Courtesy of George Merritt]

Right: One of the few pictures ever taken of Daddy without his hat. *Below:* Daddy performing at a Western Auto store opening. That's Mother behind the sunglasses waiting in the car. [Courtesy of George Merritt]

Above: Hank Williams and the Drifting Cowboys, about to leave from the "Louisiana Hayride" for a Chamber of Commerce goodwill tour through east Texas in April 1949. Standing (left to right) are Lum York, Clint Holmes, Bob McNett, Felton Pruett, and Tony Franchini. Daddy is seated. *Below:* The Shreveport Municipal Auditorium, home of the "Louisiana Hayride."

Above: Mother was a very beautiful young woman. *Right:* This is the dress I wore to the Easter picnic in 1949 with Kitty and Johnny and the other Hayride families.

Above: The house on Franklin Road the way it originally looked, complete with the opening notes to "Lovesick Blues" on the wrought-iron railing. *Below:* This was our 1949 Christmas card photo.

: Daddy and Randall
k, Jr.) on our sofa at
 in Nashville. *Below:*
er and Daddy with other
 families on the flight to
any for the "Grand Ole
"/A.J. Reynolds Tobacco
any tour in November
 Rod Brasfield and his
are in the front; behind
 Daddy is cuddled up to
er, with Roy Acuff and
ife behind them.
rtesy of Dollie Denny]

Above: Thanksgiving dinner while in Germany. Left to right are Mildred (Mrs. Roy) Acuff, Daddy, Mother, Rod Brasfield, Red Foley, and Minnie Pearl. [Courtesy of Dollie Denny] *Below:* Daddy (with his camera) and Little Jimmy Dickens on the same trip to Germany. [Courtesy of Dollie Denny]

Right: Having a new baby in the family was very exciting. *Below:* An early photo of Mother, Daddy, and me.

Robertson Academy Horse Show 1951

Above: Me on Trigger at the Robertson Academy Horse Show in
1951. It was my first horse show, and I won first place in the
costume division. *Below:* My ninth birthday party, at which Fred
Rose and Daddy sang "Happy Birthday."

mad, or madder, and picked up that glass of water and threw it at Daddy. It hit him in the head and cut him a little bit. It wasn't bad, and Daddy didn't say anything; he just picked up the glass and put it in the trash and cleaned off his cut.

Everybody was relieved and excited when Randall Hank Williams was born on May 26, 1949. Mother reminisced about Hank Jr.'s birth in 1975:

> After I finally became pregnant, which took a few years, Hank was thrilled to death. I told him not to worry about it, it's going to be a boy. In fact, my whole layette had blue in it. I didn't even have anything in solid white.
>
> When I went into the hospital, I had already been in about two or three times with false labor before Hank, Jr., was finally born. He weighed ten pounds and three ounces and practically killed the both of us.
>
> It was really a bad scene for Hank; they couldn't get him away from the door once he heard me screaming. When they tried to tell him he had a healthy son, he said, "No, I don't want to see him, I just want to see my wife." Of course, he didn't mean that. It was just that he wanted to know if I was all right, which I was.
>
> I can't tell you how happy he was after a few days. He would walk into the hospital and down to the nursery, and he felt so proud. All the people would be standing around, and of course Hank, Jr., was so much larger than all the other babies there. Hank, Sr., would proudly point out, "That's my son. Look how big he is already and imagine how big he's going to be!"

I didn't get to go to the hospital when Mother had the baby, so I was glad when they came back home. They had fixed the bassinet in their bedroom, and I remember going in there to look at him and talk to him. Mrs. Scoggins was hired to take care of Randall, as we called him. She always let me help her feed him and rock him. I took to him right away, and Daddy was so proud of him.

Mother was not what you call a doting parent. She was good to us and showed us love, but she wasn't the kind that coddled you a lot. Daddy did a lot more coddling. Mother took a lot of time with Hank, Jr., but she wasn't the type to be tied to the house because of the children. Whenever Daddy needed to go, she wanted to be able to go with him. Mother was always trying to figure out ways to make Daddy bigger or to get bigger bookings for him. She was just a business-minded woman.

CHAPTER 6

There'll Be No Change in Me

We had lived in Shreveport less than a year when Daddy got his chance to try out on the "Grand Ole Opry." He and Mother were both twenty-five years old. The skyrocketing success of "Lovesick Blues" made it impossible for them to ignore Hank Williams any longer, and he was scheduled to perform on June 11, 1949, during the 9:30 P.M. Warren Paint segment of the "Greatest Country Music Show on Earth." None of us were prepared for the changes this would bring to our lives.

Daddy had disbanded the Drifting Cowboys in late May, and Mother was still recovering from her recent childbirth, so Daddy made the trip to Nashville alone for his first appearance on the Opry stage.

When Daddy approached the microphone on the stage of the Ryman Auditorium that night, few people recognized him by sight. But as soon as he sang the first two lines of "Lovesick Blues," they exploded into wild cheers and screams. His music could barely be heard above the noise, and the fans wouldn't let him off the stage when he finished the song. They called him back for six encores!

The next Saturday night, June 18, he was part of the network segment of the Opry, and NBC broadcast him singing "Lovesick Blues" across the entire nation. Almost immediately, Hank Williams became hillbilly music's first superstar. Stepping out on that stage and singing that song was like stepping into a tidal wave.

We didn't actually move to Nashville until late summer, but

Daddy was up there a lot due to his appearances on the Opry. He also had to put his band together again. He called his old buddies Don Helms and Bob McNett, and he hired a fiddler named Jerry Rivers and Jerry's friend Hillous Butram to play bass.

Don Helms remembers Daddy's words when he called: "Meet me at the Hermitage Hotel. I always told you when I started to work on the 'Grand Ole Opry,' I was going to take your ass with me."

According to Don, they didn't practice too much before they performed for the first time.

> When I met Hank at the hotel that morning, he had Bob McNett and Jerry Rivers with him, and pretty soon Hillous came. So we jawed a little while and then went up to the room and played a little bit. Hank had us set up to go over to WSM and audition as his Opry band. There was no problem with how we sounded, and that night we appeared with Hank on the Opry. I had always heard of the "Grand Ole Opry" and Ernest Tubb and Roy Acuff and Cowboy Copas and Little Jimmy Dickens, and there they were. I was awestruck! When we went on and did our thing, I remembered back when I had told my mother, "One day this guy is going to be a big star," and I thought, "By God, he is."

Before Mother and Daddy left Louisiana, they had to settle one unresolved personal matter. Although they had reconciled and remained together after their separation the previous year, Mother had not withdrawn her original bill of complaint and a divorce had actually been granted on May 26, 1948. After Hank, Jr.'s birth exactly one year to the day later, Mother and Daddy had to face the question of his legitimacy unless they had the divorce annulled or declared "nunc pro tunc." On August 9, 1949, the Circuit Court of Montgomery, Alabama, amended their divorce decree by striking from it the paragraphs dissolving their marriage.

Life in Nashville started out to be a dream come true for Mother. Her girlhood fantasies of fame and fortune had turned to reality. She had fallen in love with a three-bedroom brick house at 4916 Franklin Road in the Oak Hill subdivision just south of Nashville. The house was situated on three acres of land out in the country, but it was only several miles down the road from the Acuff-Rose offices. Mother and Daddy purchased the property for 21,000 dollars from Mr. and Mrs. W. Raymond Denney in early September. The house was small, but Mother immediately started making plans to enlarge it.

Through the Nurse's Register in Nashville, Mother got in touch with Miss Audrey Ragland, whose specialty was caring for new mothers and their babies just out of the hospital. Miss Ragland was only four feet, nine inches tall, and I thought she looked like one of the Campbell Soup Kids. She came to work very soon after we moved, and she was there until the end. Here is her memory of how our life in Nashville started:

> Mr. and Mrs. Williams had lived in Nashville about three weeks when I went to work for them in September of 1949. Randall was four months old, and Lycrecia was eight years old. The first time I met them, Mrs. Williams picked me up in front of the Maxwell House Hotel. She took me back to their house out in the country, and I was to babysit while they went out to dinner. Randall and Lycrecia's aunt Lynette was there, too. Then a couple of weeks later they called me again. The third time I went, Mr. Williams asked me if I'd move out there and stay with them, and I did.
>
> It was the original house; nothing had been added then, and we were a little crowded. I slept in the original den, next to Mr. and Mrs. Williams' room. Lycrecia was very sweet and shy. She always stood back. I guess I wasn't as attentive to her as I should have been, but Randall demanded attention and she didn't. Consequently he got more attention than she did. At first Lycrecia didn't have any friends and it was pretty hard for her, but next door was the Harlan family. She got acquainted with their children, Howard and Susan, and they had a lot of fun.
>
> I didn't even know who Mr. Williams was when I went to work for them. I asked Lycrecia, "What does your Daddy do?" and she said, "My Daddy's Hank Williams. He's a country music singer," but that didn't mean anything to me.

That fall, work started on the first addition to our new house. A new master bedroom, den, breezeway, and two-car garage were built off the kitchen and living room. Now, everyone, including Miss Ragland, had their own room. Mother also

designed a wrought-iron railing for the front of the house, decorated with the notes from the first few bars of "Lovesick
Blues." It got a lot of attention.

Dollie Denny, who later married the Opry manager Jim
Denny, was a dancer and sold souvenir books at the Ryman
when Mother and Daddy came to Nashville. She recalls first
seeing them sitting close together on a bench backstage at the
Opry. Mother wore very little make-up, her hair was long and
straight, and she was dressed simply, with no frills. "However,"
Dollie adds, "Audrey was a fast learner. She started buying
silver and china and fixing the house up and going first class.
This little girl from Alabama just blossomed out."

As the wife of a country music superstar, Mother started
giving a lot of attention to making a showcase for Daddy: buying the house and decorating it, dressing in style, and planning
social activities. She ordered custom Western outfits for herself, for Daddy, and for the Drifting Cowboys from Nudie's
Rodeo Tailors of California. That introduced the "Nudie
Look," the flashy, sequined, embroidered Western suit fashion,
to Nashville. She started shopping at Weinburger's, an exclusive shop that sold seven-hundred to two-thousand-dollar
dresses back in 1950. She decorated our home in a modern
style, using Oriental furniture and accents instead of the typical "country-look" furnishings.

Don Helms says that "some of the women in Nashville didn't
like Audrey because she always dressed nicer than they did,
and some of the men didn't like her because they felt like, 'Hell,
you can't ever get to Hank anymore without going through
Audrey.' Audrey was maybe overdressed sometimes, but she
looked so much sharper than anybody else. She had very expensive clothes, and some women that can't have that don't like
it. And I don't recall that she ever refused to let anyone see
Hank, but I think people thought that and built barriers themselves."

For years Mother had been an active partner in Daddy's musical career, and now she wanted to share the glory and continue to help build his image and prestige. Her involvement
was no different than before, but Daddy's new status made
people look at her a lot differently.

Jerry Rivers, Daddy's fiddle player, remembers a time when

Daddy was ignoring his career and Mother was trying to keep him on track.

> My wife, June, and Hank and I were fishing one time down off Rudy's dock at Richland Creek on Kentucky Lake, and Audrey chartered an amphibious airplane to come and land on the lake and pick Hank up. We were crappie fishing — we always did that in the spring — and they had been invited to some kind of dinner or function that Hank had forgotten all about.
>
> She was the drive in his business because he didn't like most of it. Sometimes he didn't even want to go to the Opry on Saturday nights. He'd raise hell about it when she would tell him what he needed to do, but later that's the way he'd go, and most of the time she was right. Then everyone would say, "Poor Hank, what a great guy and a great singer, and Audrey did him like that."
>
> It quickly became obvious that Hank was getting a stature that no one in country music had ever had before, and it was easier for Audrey to deal with than him. Audrey saw Minnie Pearl and others beginning to be part of Nashville society rather than just some hillbilly that picks a guitar and his nose. Audrey'd rather be at the country club, and Hank would rather be down on the riverbank fishing. Now who's right, and who's wrong? It's not a matter of right and wrong, but you have a little bit of a clash there.

Mother was a little too ambitious, maybe. Maybe she wanted things a little too fast for Daddy, and he just wanted to let them kind of happen. If they happened, fine, but if they didn't, that was all right, too, whereas Mother wanted to promote. She wanted to let everybody see what he could do. Even though I think Daddy needed that direction, he would have wanted her just to be a plain little housewife and stay home. But Mother couldn't do that. She did that in her first marriage, and her husband ran off and left her when she was pregnant. I think she realized, too, that if she had stayed at home being the good little wife, Daddy wouldn't have gone any further with his talent. He enjoyed singing, but I think he wanted to be able to hunt and fish, too.

Daddy's first studio session after joining the Opry was on August 30 in Cincinnati, Ohio, when he recorded "I'm So Lonesome I Could Cry," "A House Without Love (Is Not A Home)," "I Just Don't Like This Kind of Living," and "My Bucket's Got A Hole In It."

Then, in October — on two consecutive Sundays — Mother and Daddy and the Drifting Cowboys recorded a series of eight fifteen-minute programs called "The Health and Happiness Shows." The plan was to release the programs to promote the patent medicine Hadacol, and later to sell the shows to another sponsor. Excerpts of the shows were eventually released commercially by MGM.

The next month, on November 13, a group of Opry people, including Mother and Daddy, left on a tour sponsored by the U.S. Air Force. They went to entertain military and civilian personnel stationed on U.S. bases in Germany, Austria, England, the Azores, and Bermuda. They were gone for two weeks. Two weeks is a long time to an eight-year-old girl left with someone she doesn't know very well.

Unlike Mrs. Scoggins, Miss Ragland would never let me change Randall or feed him. She spent all her time with him, and I used to wonder why she didn't like me. I soon learned not to ask her to do much for me.

Besides Mother and Daddy, the entertainment package for the tour included Rod Brasfield, Minnie Pearl, Roy Acuff and his Smoky Mountain Boys, Red Foley and his band, and Little Jimmy Dickens. Most of the performers' spouses accompanied them, as did announcer Grant Turner and Opry Vice President and General Manager Harry Stone.

Grant Turner remembers that "they worked us to death. They'd have us up in the morning early and there was usually some kind of morning activity. At 11:30, no matter where we were, we went to the bar and then to lunch. In the afternoon, we'd have a hospital tour. Then it'd be back to the bar about 5:00, followed by dinner and the show that night. That was our routine. We were going all the time. Finally the husbands and wives all got mad at each other. We had some really knockdowns and dragouts."

More and more, Mother began to stay at home when Daddy went out on the road. Miss Ragland says the main reason she was hired was because Mother wanted to go out on the road with Daddy. Although she did for a while, it eventually became too much of a drag to go out with him all the time. Daddy liked her to go because he wanted to be with her, and she wanted to be with him, too, but she still wanted to be at home with her children. The pressure was hard on her, and Miss Ragland says she was miserable sometimes on account of it.

As Miss Ragland explains, "Mr. Williams would be gone during the week. But he'd call all the time, and sometimes they would fight over the phone. When he came back for the Saturday night Opry, that's when they needed me the most because they liked to be out and together. She'd be expecting certain things from him when he came home, and he was usually very tired. He'd try to make up for the time he wasn't there, but he'd be expecting certain things from her too. It was true love; it just was a strain on them to be separated.

Daddy was not used to so many demands on his time or such pressure to work and travel from so many different people. Now it was the Opry, the promoters, the journalists, MGM Records, the fans—they all claimed their right to a piece of him.

On December 8, 1949, Daddy and the Drifting Cowboys, Cowboy Copas, Annie Lou and Danny (Dill), Hank Garland, Lazy Jim Day, Elton Britt, and the Duke of Paducah began a week-long engagement at the Hippodrome Theater in Baltimore, Maryland. Jerry Rivers remembers the occasion as his first experience with Daddy's falling off the wagon. When it became obvious that Daddy had begun to drink, the promoter of the Baltimore show hired yodeler Elton Britt to watch over him. Then one of the square dance girls hid liquor miniatures in her hoop skirt and slipped them to Daddy. So the promoter, Oscar Davis, sent for Mother.

Don Helms and Bob McNett picked Mother up at the airport and brought her back to the hotel. "Sitting in the lobby of the hotel there in Baltimore, I was talking to Audrey," says Bob. "She said, 'I am so upset and discouraged, I think I've lost the love I had for Hank.' I didn't believe her then, and I still don't. But right at that point you could see there was such a strain on that marriage. It was very important to her for him not to drink. I think their love never really did disappear, though, in spite of all that happened."

Bob McNett also remembers a comment Daddy made to him that week about his new son. "You don't know what it's like to have a Bocephus waiting for you at home," he said. Daddy had taken to calling Randall "Bocephus," an affectionate name he borrowed from a puppet used by Opry comedian Rod Brasfield.

Daddy was back in the Castle Studios on January 9, 1950, to record "Long Gone Lonesome Blue," "Why Don't You Love Me (Like You Used To Do)," "Why Should We Try Anymore," and "My Son Calls Another Man Daddy." The next day, January 10, Daddy recorded the first of his spiritual/philosophic recitation numbers, "Too Many Parties And Too Many Pals," "Beyond The Sunset," "The Funeral," and "Everything's Okay," but he recorded them under the name of Luke the Drifter.

According to Don Helms, "Hank pushed hard to do those records. The problem for MGM and Fred Rose was that things like "The Funeral" would not go on a jukebox, and when the *Billboard* would come out with 'New Hank Williams Release,' the jukebox operators wouldn't pay any attention to the titles. They'd buy a thousand of them, and then they'd have a thousand duds for their jukeboxes. But Hank wanted to do stuff like that, so MGM and Fred decided to let him do it, but under a different name."

The fact that Daddy was Luke the Drifter was never a secret. Once his fans knew who Luke was, they thought it was funny and rushed out to buy his latest record just the same.

Everybody knew Daddy really cared about people. His heart went out to the downtrodden and the handicapped and the lost souls of the world. He thought as Luke the Drifter he could express his understanding of the pain and despair in the life of the ordinary person and maybe bring some comfort to a few of those lost souls along the way.

I know from my experience that Daddy was a compassionate man. I don't know what he was like out on the road, but he wasn't ever short-tempered or ill with me, and we spent a lot of time together.

He liked to bowl, and we went to the bowling alley in Melrose, near the Acuff-Rose offices, quite a lot. I was too young to pick up the regular-size ball, so he bought me one that was smaller and lighter and had my initials put on it. Fred Peyser, who owned the camera shop downstairs from the Melrose Theater, remembered going bowling with Daddy once and said he was an excellent bowler. Daddy didn't keep score, Mr. Peyser said, but he got a lot of strikes and spares that day.

I had a very good childhood those first years in Nashville. Of the two of us, Hank, Jr., and me, I feel I'm the lucky one. I may not be Daddy's blood daughter, but I got to do a lot more and go more places with Daddy than Hank, Jr., ever did.

Not a lot of men would take a nine- or ten-year-old girl fishing, but I remember one time Daddy took me with him to Kentucky Lake. We left before daylight and met some other people up there. Daddy and I were in one boat, and the other people were in a separate boat. We sat there all day long.

By noon I was ready to come home. We weren't catching anything, but Daddy was a die-hard fisherman. He kept saying, "Oh no, Honey, we're fixing to catch some, just the very next throw, we'll get us one. You just need to be real quiet." I'd sigh and say, "O.K., Daddy."

Later in the day, I saw a snake swimming toward the boat. Daddy took the paddle and killed it, but it scared me so bad, I really wanted to go home then.

We had the average family, in my opinion. We ate breakfast together, and we sat down to supper together. Mother cooked some, but she didn't do all of it because a maid helped her by then. We got a TV sometime in 1950, after Daddy had seen the one at our next-door neighbors, the Harlans. We spent most of our time at home together in the den. We just talked about things that normal people talk about, nothing significant. Mother would ask me, "Honey, have you got your homework done?" And if I needed some help, she would try to help me with it. Daddy never did because he only finished the eighth or ninth grade, but he always asked me how I was doing.

Daddy liked to joke around when he was at home. He would come in and grab me around the neck and scrub the top of my head. We'd get down on the living room floor before Hank, Jr., went to bed, and all three of us would wrestle around and play. He never left me out. He always seemed to feel good and never complained, even though he had a lot of trouble with his back and was often in pain.

Mother and Daddy normally sat together on the sofa. He would put his arm around her and hug her. Daddy was a very affectionate man, more openly affectionate than Mother.

Mother was a little reserved out in public or when anybody was around. She was not cold, but she was not as openly affectionate.

A long time ago, people just didn't think you were supposed to show affection in front of children, and that's the way Mother's mama and daddy raised her. Now Daddy was not vulgar or anything, but he would kiss her on the cheek or give her a little hug. She didn't push him away, but if he got a little too amorous, she probably said, "Not in front of the kids."

Mother had a very authoritative voice, but she didn't yell at us kids. When we misbehaved, she'd just give us a pop on the fanny as we went by and say, "Don't do that anymore." Daddy never whipped me, and he seldom scolded me. I don't ever remember him even scolding Hank, Jr., when he was a baby, either.

There was a lot of happiness in my childhood. I had the love of two parents who were both extremely good to me. As I got older, they did fuss some, but if they disagreed or had an argument, it was usually done away from me. All married couples argue some. I know that Mother was hot-tempered, more so than Daddy was, but I don't remember that she picked on him all the time like some people say she did. And I don't think two people ever loved each other more than they loved each other.

I can't recall that a lot of entertainers came over to the house when we were small. Occasionally, one or two would come in, but it was no big deal. They just sat around and talked with Mother and Daddy. If they came over to write, they didn't do it around me.

I used to go up to the Acuff-Rose offices with Daddy quite often, and I remember Wendell in the mailroom was always so nice to me. He let me help him sort the mail, and I thought that was just the greatest thing in the world.

Daddy called Fred Rose "Pappy" and respected him as a businessman. In return, Mr. Rose said he deeply valued "one thing Hank had — and all his friends recognized it . . . loyalty. I don't give a hang whether he drank or not. I appreciate the fact that he was loyal. I know that one time another firm tried to bribe him away from me for fifty thousand dollars, but he stuck with Rose. He'd say, 'I started with Rose and I'll stay with Rose.' And he did."

Most of the time, Daddy and Fred Rose worked over at Fred's little home studio because he had his piano over there. And Daddy traveled so much that his visits to the office were usually brief.

In addition to all Mother was doing with adding on to the house and promoting Daddy's career, she recorded seven sides for Decca Records with Daddy and the Drifting Cowboys on March 28 and April 1, 1950. Three of the songs, "My Tight-Wad Daddy," "Model-T-Love" and "I Like That Kind" were her own compositions. Then she did two of Daddy's religious numbers, "Help Me Understand" and "How Can You Refuse Him Now," as well as one of his earlier releases, "Honky-Tonkin'." "What Put The Pep in Grandma," a romping, stomping kind of song about Hadacol rounded out the sessions.

Mother enjoyed singing. She had been a part of Daddy's stage show since the early years of their marriage, in the mid-1940s, and she always wanted to be a part of what Daddy was doing. She enjoyed the limelight, the attention, but she was not a very good singer. She couldn't keep time, and that aggravated Daddy. He wasn't exactly a perfectionist, yet he didn't have a lot of patience when it came to singing. I think Daddy had mixed emotions about the whole affair, because Mother was a pretty woman and he rather enjoyed having her on the stage with him to show her off.

The subject of Mother's singing had always been a minor point of contention, but Daddy usually tried his best to make her happy on this issue. He brought her on the Opry stage to sing gospel duets with him, he included her in the same way on his radio programs and in the studio, and he arranged the Decca recording contract for her. Over the years, her singing ability never really improved, though, so the Decca releases didn't meet with much success.

"I never heard her say, 'Now, you've got to put me on, you've got to put me on!'" recalls Don Helms. "She was just always there and ready to go on and sometimes he would call her up. When he did, she was proud and tried her best."

Dollie Denny remembers one Saturday when Daddy and Mother had had an argument. Daddy called Jim Denny and told him he didn't want Mother on the show that night. "Then, by the time showtime came around," Dollie continues, "they'd made up, so he had to call back and say she was on again. And that's the way it was. Whatever Hank wanted. If he wanted her, she was there; if they were on the outs, she wasn't. He didn't think she had the greatest voice in the world, but she loved to do it. That was a form of punishment, you see. If he said, 'No, you can't sing tonight,' well, she didn't get to sing. It was just that simple because he had the upper hand there."

I can now see that Daddy and Mother were both strong-minded, stubborn people, especially in relation to each other. They were even childish at times.

One time at breakfast, we were all sitting in the kitchen, and Mother and Daddy got to talking about buying new cars. Mother wanted a convertible, a yellow-gold one, and Daddy said, "You don't need a convertible. You're a married woman and don't have any business with a convertible."

Mother said, "I don't care. I want a convertible, and that's what I'm going to get." She got it, too, and Daddy got that green limousine, the long car that he traveled in. Mother always had convertibles after that.

"I remember Hank came out to see me after he had just bought his new cars," Don Helms recalls. "I had just bought a house and my first new car, too. There we both were, we'd never had anything and now I had a new car, a new home, a good job, and Hank was famous. And he just was feeling kind of humble and said, 'Shag, we've come a hell of a long way, haven't we?' and I said, 'Yeah, we sure have.' He never stopped to put in perspective how big he was getting at the time. He just knew he had money coming in and a big handful was a lot of money and a little handful was a little money. That's the way he put it."

CHAPTER 7

Ain't Nothin' Ever Gonna Be Alright Nohow

The day before my ninth birthday, August 13, 1950, I had a big party at our house. A lot of little girls in party dresses came, and Fred Rose and Daddy sang "Happy Birthday" to me. I received a very special present that I had been asking for all year — a horse! Daddy had bought me a five-gaited, black-and-white spotted pony named Trigger from Mr. and Mrs. Ray Garrett.

Ruth Garrett, Ray's wife, remembers that the first time she saw Mother and Daddy, "they had come to a horse show at the old fairgrounds to look for a pony for Lycrecia. They were dressed in these white, ultra-suede Western clothes with the fringe on the sleeve — just an elegant couple. Ray got to talking to Hank and told him we had just the pony for his little girl."

Mr. and Mrs. Garrett and their children, Mark and Freda, brought the pony out to the house in the trailer for my birthday. Freda remembers that Mother brought them each a piece of cake on a napkin with some red party punch. I was overwhelmed with my new horse, and when the Garretts had to take it back because we didn't have any place to keep it yet, I raised cain about that.

The only time I remember Daddy ever raising his voice to me was the day of that party. We were standing in the dining room with a lot of people around, and I kept trying to get his attention. I kept saying, "Daddy, Daddy!" but he was busy talking. Finally, I just popped up and shouted, "Hank!" Well, he looked around immediately and said, "What'd you call me?" I said, "Daddy." And he said, "That's right, and don't you ever let me hear you call me 'Hank' again."

At the beginning, we kept Trigger out at the Garretts, and I started going over there regularly so I could ride. Miss Ragland or Mother would usually drive me over there, but sometimes Daddy would take me and maybe stay a little while if I had something to show him. Later, he had a barn and ring built behind our house and hired Albert Wilson to teach me how to ride.

We had a lot of fun with Trigger. Daddy would rent a horse trailer, and we would enter Trigger in the shows around Nashville. The horse shows always had a costume class, and Mother had Nudie of California make me a cowgirl outfit. It was a white shirt and pants with red trim and a white hat. Daddy bought me a red saddle and bridle to match. He was so proud whenever I won a prize in my class.

Freda Garrett Moon remembers Daddy was friendlier than most of her other friends' fathers.

He had a very warm personality and would talk to you. He didn't put you off like a lot of parents did. One time I was over there, and Audrey had told us we had to go to bed because it was getting late. It was a Saturday night, and Hank was working the Opry. Lycrecia wanted to talk to him about the horse or something, so we decided to stay up. After Audrey went to bed, we came back in the den and sat up until he got home. We were whispering because Audrey's bedroom was right behind the den, and we sat there just wishing the clock would tick off and the Opry would be over. When he came in, he had on a white suit with rhinestones and sparkles and glitter. I remember he was real nice, and Lycrecia got whatever it was that she wanted.

Daddy bought himself a strawberry roan Tennessee Walking Horse named High Life. Walking horses are supposed to be very smooth riding, and he thought maybe it wouldn't jar his back so bad. He could never ride very much though, so I used to ride High Life for him.

For some reason, Trigger did not want you to mount on his

right side, the correct side, but you could get on his left side. If you tried to mount as you were supposed to, he'd just back around into you. Daddy was down at the ring one day, and he was bound and determined to get on Trigger on the correct side. He was wearing the pointed-toe cowboy boots that he always wore. Trigger kept backing into him, and Daddy was getting mad. I suggested, "Well, Daddy, why don't you just get on the other side of him. It's no big deal."

"No," he insisted, "this is the side you're supposed to get on, and I'm getting on this side." Finally, he just hauled off and kicked Trigger in the stomach with his boot. And Trigger stood still and let him get on.

That made me so mad. I didn't say a word, but I thought it was being cruel for no reason. It was the only time that I ever saw Daddy get mad and lose his temper fooling with the horses. Normally, he was so easy-going, but now, looking back, I realize that his back was probably hurting him at the time and made him short-tempered.

Part of it might have been that Daddy was keeping up a furious pace throughout 1950. He did personal appearance tours from coast to coast and even into Canada; he did a daily morning radio show on WSM whenever he was in town; he did the "Duckhead Work Clothes" show on Saturday afternoons, and then the "Grand Ole Opry" on Saturday nights.

And there were three more recording sessions that year in the Castle Studio. His June 14 session was brief, consisting of only two songs, "They'll Never Take Her Love From Me" and "Honky Tonk Blues." On August 31, he recorded "Nobody's Lonesome For Me," "Moanin' The Blues," "Help Me Understand," and Fred Rose's warning to Joseph Stalin, "No, No, Joe." The last two numbers were attributed to Luke the Drifter. His last 1950 session, on December 21, included "Cold, Cold Heart," "Dear John," "Just Waitin'," and "Men With Broken Hearts." Again, Daddy used his Luke the Drifter alias for the second pair of songs.

Daddy began 1951 with a tour through Oklahoma and Texas accompanied by his friend, Little Jimmy Dickens. Jimmy has a lot of fond memories of working with Daddy.

Hank just liked me. We were two different types of acts, but we had a lot of respect for each other. He liked the way I performed because he told Jerry and the other guys in the band many times, "We have to watch that little devil out there!" He's the one that nicknamed me "Tater" after my song, "Take An Old Cold Tater."

I flew a lot of miles with him and Minnie Pearl and Minnie's husband, Henry Cannon. Hank wrote "Hey, Good-Lookin'," and "Howlin' At the Moon" going to Wichita Falls, Texas, on Henry's plane.

He sure got a big kick out of kidding me up at the "Grand Ole Opry" when we did the Friday Night Frolic from the old insurance building. He came in there and said, "I recorded your song today, Tater." That was only about a week after he told me he was writing "Hey, Good-Lookin'" for me, and it was going to be a hit. We just laughed about it. He said, "That's too good a song for you anyway." He loved to kid me. He'd pull the curtain back when we were playing a concert and say, "Look out there, Tater. You drew me a good crowd."

The thing that amazed me the most about him was his ability to put those words together. When an idea hit him, he could put it down in ten or fifteen minutes, I saw him. He'd say, "Got a piece of paper, Tater? Take this down." Then he'd sit there and reel those lines off. They just knocked me out because every line seemed to get a little stronger.

When he performed, he didn't have to work the stage. All he had to do was stand there and bend his knees and bow his back up a little bit in a suit that didn't fit him, and the crowds went wild. Mr. Nudie made his clothes, but Hank could wear the most expensive suit and it'd look like a sack because of the way he put it on.

He'd wear a dress tie with a Western suit, which didn't work, and he'd tie those real old-fashioned long knots. The tie would be off the side and I'd straighten it up for him before he went out on the stage, but he'd pull it right back over there and say, "You're too particular." He figured those old country boys that came to see him would like him the way he was. He hoped they did because it suited him.

When we were in Oklahoma City, he and I went shopping in this department store and it had a Western section. He saw some cufflinks that were replicas of .45 pistols, and he loved those cufflinks. They were real expensive. They had little pearl handles and all. He asked the man, "How many of these cufflinks you got?" The guy said, "We have a lot of them." Hank said, "That's what I want. I want a lot of them." The guy said, "Well, we probably have a gross. You don't want that many." He said, "I'll take a gross." He bought twelve dozen pairs of cufflinks with little pistols. I had no idea what he did with all of them. He probably gave them away. They must have cost him a fortune.

He'd call me at home a lot and I'd come out and visit with him. We'd just sit and talk about nothing in particular. He was very moody. His moods were probably related to alcohol, although I never saw him drinking and I never saw him drunk. I know what he went through to be an alcoholic, and it's very, very difficult when you drink as much as I did or he did, not to take that first drink before you go on that stage. It's difficult for a person who gets used to that. It becomes a part of what you do.

As Mother reflected many years later:

Hank was a very, very shy person, and not really sure of himself except when he walked out on the stage. He was extremely nervous before each performance, and each time he went on the stage, it'd take him about three minutes to really relax. The audience wouldn't see it, but I would know it and he would know it. I think most performers are like that, and I think when you lose that, you've lost it all.

He was a loner. Well, it was really shyness and loneliness together. He could be doing a show, and before he went on stage or after he came off, you'd see him sitting over in a corner. He might be on a package show with a number of other artists, and he'd be sitting alone just picking his guitar and singing.

Of course, he was a genius at writing. He was a very brilliant person, even though he only had an eighth grade education. But no matter what our strengths might be, we're all weak in some vein. Even kings and queens and lords have their weaknesses, you know.

On March 16 Daddy recorded "I Can't Help It (If I'm Still In Love With You)," "Howling' At The Moon," "Hey, Good-Lookin'," and "My Heart Would Know." One week later, on March 23, he and Mother recorded two gospel duets, "The Pale Horse and His Rider" and "A Home In Heaven." On June 1 he recorded four songs: "Ramblin' Man," "Pictures From Life's Other Side," "I've Been Down That Road Before," and "I Dreamed About Mama Last Night" as Luke the Drifter.

The big thing I remember happening in 1951 was the grand opening of Hank and Audrey's Corral on June 16. The store was Mother's enterprising idea, inspired by the growing interest in the Western-style look that she and Daddy helped to make popular in Nashville. It was Nashville's first Western apparel store, at 724 Commerce Street, just two doors down from the Ernest Tubb Record Shop.

The Corral had a big neon sign, decorated with pictures of Daddy and Mother. The storefront was designed to create a feeling of the old West, with rustic wood panelling and a wagon-wheel lamp over the entrance. Inside, clothes and other items hung from racks and more wagon-wheels. The various souvenirs for sale included custom-made Hank and Audrey dolls.

The opening was broadcast over WSM from 5:00 to 5:30 P.M. I can remember a lot of people at the opening. They were excited to get to meet Mother and Daddy and talk to them personally.

Mother hired Mac McGee in late 1950 or early 1951 to operate the store. He eventually bought it, one year after the grand opening. Mr. McGee remembers the Corral was a hangout for Nashville musicians, including six or seven down-on-their-luck "regulars." Mother and Daddy would often stop by, pull some money out of the cash register, and send someone down to the nearby Krystal to buy hamburgers for everyone. They were also known to give away cash or clothing to needy friends and acquaintances. McGee says, "Both Hank and Audrey had the most charitable hearts of anyone you've ever seen."

It was really exciting to go in there and be able to say, "Mother, I want this right here" and have her say, "O.K., Honey, go ahead and take it if you like it."

The opening was so popular that Mother and Daddy started broadcasting the "Hank and Audrey" show live from the Corral every Saturday evening at the same time. They stopped after three months because the crowds became too big to manage.

Daddy had always loved his radio audiences, and they felt the same way about him. He had worked off and on for over seven years on WSFA in Montgomery, where he claimed, "I got the popularist daytime program on this station." Fans mobbed the studio morning and afternoon just to shake

Daddy's hand or get his autograph, and once when somebody at the station got the idea that nobody listened to his kind of music, Daddy decided to conduct a little experiment. "I told everybody on the radio that this was my last program. 'If anybody's enjoyed it,' I said, 'I'd like to hear from 'em.' I got four hundred cards and letters that afternoon and the next mornin' . . . They decided they wanted to keep my kind 'a music."

Later, on his "Johnny Fair Syrup" show in Shreveport, Daddy proved that a lot of people listened to him when he sold enough syrup to bring the company out of the red.

By the time we moved to Nashville, Daddy was an eight-year veteran of radio at the age of twenty-five. He appeared weekly on Saturday mornings on a show sponsored by Duck-head work clothes and also had a daily show at 7:15 A.M. sponsored by Mother's Best flour. The transcription discs for this weekday show are a precious memory of Daddy's sense of humor and quick wit because they were all done without scripts. It makes me both happy and sad to listen to Daddy's voice and the sound of his laughter.

Early in 1951, Fred Rose and his son, Wes, and Murray Nash, who was Mr. Rose's right-hand man, had begun their efforts to introduce Daddy's songs into the pop marketplace. Murray had some connections to Perry Como and Mitch Miller, but neither were open to "hillbilly" music. Finally, both agreed to meet with Fred and Wes Rose in New York. The main song they wanted to push was "Cold, Cold Heart," so they took a semi-pop demo of the song with them instead of Daddy's "country" version.

Out of that trip came Tony Bennett's beautiful, orchestrated version of the song. It hit the pop charts in July 1951 and was one of Bennett's first smash hits. According to Jerry Rivers, Daddy couldn't get enough of the record and played it over and over whenever he found it on a jukebox.

On July 25, 1951, Daddy recorded "I'd Still Want You," "Lonesome Whistle," "Crazy Heart," and "Baby, We're Really in Love." Sixteen days later, August 10, he recorded "I'm Sorry for You, My Friend" and "Half As Much"; he also recut "I'd Still Want You," and "Baby, We're Really in Love." Both sessions were at Studio D (Castle Studios) in Nashville.

In October, *Billboard* reported that Daddy "has blossomed out as a full-fledged pop writer." By then Frankie Laine and Jo Stafford and Tennessee Ernie and Helen O'Connell had done "Hey, Good-Lookin'" for different labels; Guy Mitchell had released "I Can't Help It" on Columbia; Kay Starr had done "Lovesick Blues" for Capitol; and Polly Bergen and Theresa Brewer had both cut "Honky-Tonkin'."

Daddy's career was peaking throughout the summer of 1951. His pop chart successes were stretching his reputation outside the pure hillbilly markets and spreading his name across the entire United States and even into Canada and overseas.

Back in the city where it all began, Montgomery, Alabama, Mayor W. A. Gayle proclaimed July fifteenth "Hank Williams Homecoming Day." The celebration was sponsored by the Montgomery Junior Chamber of Commerce and was to be the first big show ever held at the brand-new, two million-dollar Cow Coliseum. Nine thousand people turned out to see the "Grand Ole Opry" cast, including Mother and Daddy, Hank Snow, and the Carter Family featuring guitarist Chet Atkins. Mrs. Stone and Mother both received bouquets as part of the homecoming ceremony, and the Jaycees presented Daddy with a gold watch for his contributions as "Alabama's Goodwill Ambassador."

Brack Schuffert, who was part of the program, remembers that Daddy was sitting backstage waiting to go on when a young boy walked up to him and asked, "Hank, how about letting me be on your show today."

Daddy said, "Son, I'm sorry, but I've already got my program made out."

The boy said, "Aw Hank, all I do is sing your songs. Please let me sing just one song on your show today."

Daddy thought a minute and said, "Well, OK, I'll let you sing one. What are you doing to do?"

"I want to sing 'Hey, Good-Lookin'.'"

Daddy said, "Well, that's my current song. I was planning on plugging that myself."

"Aw Hank, let me sing it," the boy begged.

Daddy gave in. "All right, go ahead," he said. "I'll just sing something else."

Not many stars would have done anything like that. The

coincidence is that the boy was Lamar Morris, who had won a talent contest to be on the show, and who later would become my husband.

I think Daddy's participation in the Hadacol Caravan in the late summer of 1951 was both a high point and a turning point in his career. It was a world apart from the medicine show circuit Daddy was traveling at the time he met Mother in 1943. The Hadacol Caravan was ultimately considered the greatest of all medicine shows. The Caravan shows had a dazzling array of big name performers, circus acts, beauty queens, and firework extravaganzas. Admission was "free" for the price of two Hadacol box tops per adult and one per child.

In mid-August 1951 Daddy and his Drifting Cowboys, accompanied by rhythm guitarist "Big" Bill Lister, drove down to Lafayette, Louisiana, to join up with the Caravan. After the one hundred and fifty crew members and entertainers had completed a full dress rehearsal before the Hadacol plant employees and local residents, the Caravan train was under way by August 15. They were to cover eighteen states throughout the South and Midwest in forty consecutive one-night stands. The acts in the unusual variety show came from every known area of music, comedy, dancing, and acrobatic entertainment.

Jerry Rivers described how popular Daddy was on the Caravan in his book, *Hank Williams, From Life to Legend*. "At first I wondered where a Tennessee fiddler would fit into all this, but I soon learned that once again I was underestimating Hank Williams' booming popularity and uncanny hypnosis of even the largest audience."

In Louisville, Kentucky, Bob Hope's guest appearance (for which he was paid a reported ten thousand dollars) earned him the unfortunate position of closing the show immediately following Daddy's performance. The thirty thousand people who packed the baseball stadium gave Daddy such a thunderous ovation that the emcee wasn't able to introduce Hope. Finally, Hope was brought onto the stage unannounced. When the applause began to die down, Hope pulled a large cowboy hat down over his ears and quipped, "Hello, folks, this is Hank Hope . . ."

No expense was spared for the participants of the Hadacol

Caravan. They traveled in nineteen Pullman cars, ate sirloin steak in the dining car, had their clothes laundered and dry-cleaned, and partook of "refreshments" in the luxurious club car, all compliments of the Hadacol organization. It is no surprise that Jerry Rivers heard that operating expenses approached ten thousand dollars a day and that the total cost for the forty days was close to one million dollars.

However, it turned out that the pay was not too good. When the Hadacol train pulled into Montgomery, Alabama, Daddy's old friend, Brack Schuffert, went down to the train station to see his friend. He remembers it this way.

> He was sitting there laid back, and I sat down right beside him and said, "Hank, how're you doing, boy?"
>
> He said, "Brack, I'm not doing too good." It was right about sundown and he said, "You know, this is the lonesomest time of the day."
>
> I looked out and saw some of those pretty movie stars and said, "Boy, what are you talking about being lonesome? All these pretty women on the train, and you're lonesome?"
>
> He said, "I don't want to have nothing to do with them folks. They think they're better than I am."
>
> I said, "Hank, don't you never think that. You're better'n every one of them that walked by."
>
> Then he pulled out a large pink check for seventy-five hundred dollars from Senator LeBlanc and said, "Looky here, Brack. Everybody on this train has got one of these checks that just bounced and come back."

The Caravan played its last show in Dallas, Texas, in mid-September, short of its original forty-day schedule. LeBlanc had sold the interests in Hadacol to a New York company, which later filed for bankruptcy.

During the nearly six-week tour of the Hadacol Caravan, Daddy and Minnie Pearl had flown back to Nashville several times to play the Saturday night Opry. "When Hank would return from these trips to Nashville," Jerry Rivers writes, "he seemed upset, and I learned that things at home were not as they had been and Hank was experiencing a breach with his family . . . Hank's popularity and fame continued to grow, but

Hank Williams, the man, was becoming more involved in twisted personal and mental conflict which was seriously affecting his home life as well as his business activities."

A review of Daddy's performances and activities during the months following the Hadacol Caravan up to the end of 1951 gives little indication of the downward slide his health and personal life were taking.

"The thing that amazed me," says Grant Turner, "was the way that he could get out and go all day long and all night long. He was on the move all the time. I never knew when Hank rested, really."

Brack Schuffert would sometimes come up from Montgomery to visit Daddy for the weekend. He recalls that Daddy never let up for more than a few minutes. He would get into town very early Saturday morning and go right over to Acuff-Rose to turn in his money and check. The publishing company was going twenty-four hours a day, seven days a week, printing Hank Williams songs and songbooks. From Acuff-Rose, Daddy would come home to eat, and from there, Fred Rose or someone from MGM would need to see him. He might be home for a little bit after that; then it was down to the National Life Building for the pre-Opry show. After the Opry's two shows, spanning from eight until midnight, he'd be ready to go to the airport to start his week on the road all over again.

Brack remembers seeing Mother outside once in the car with Hank, Jr. "When Hank, Jr., saw his daddy, he come climbing out that window on the driver's side, and Hank grabbed him and tears were just running down Hank's cheeks. He was just crying out loud. Then he had to give the baby back to Audrey and get on that plane and leave. That's just not right; it'll kill you."

        o   o   o   o   o

> Little Bocephus, you're the one
> Makes me feel good inside.
> Just to know that you're my son
> Makes my heart swell with pride.

        o   o   o   o   o

On September 24, 1951, *The Nashville Banner* announced that

Daddy had signed a five-year movie contract with Joe Paster-
nak at MGM. According to *Billboard*, Daddy was supposed to
"get straight dramatic and singing roles in featured dramatic
and musical productions. It's estimated that his salary will be
graduated up to five thousand dollars per week if he makes
good." None of that ever came to pass, however, because of the
things that soon happened in Daddy's life.

Daddy's personal appearance schedule that fall included
tours through Mississippi, Georgia, Alabama, Pennsylvania,
Ohio, and Michigan. Every Saturday night, though, no matter
how far away he had been, he was back in Nashville for the
"Grand Ole Opry." Mother still joined him sometimes on the
broadcast. While he was in town, he would perform or record
his early morning "Mother's Best" shows on WSM.

On November 14 he sang "Hey Good-Lookin'" on the Perry
Como television show on CBS from New York City. On De-
cember 11 he recorded his last session of the year, singing, "I'm
Sorry For You, My Friend," "Honky Tonk Blues," and "Let's
Turn Back The Years."

Although Daddy did not have many problems with alcohol
during 1949 through 1951, Don Helms still recalls taking
Daddy several times a year to "the Hut" outside Nashville to
dry out.

"He'd just get stoned out of his mind for a few days and we'd
usually put him in 'the Hut,'" says Helms. "The Madison Sanitarium had these little cottages for patients, and Hank'd call the
place 'the Hut.'"

> Sometimes we'd come in off a thousand mile trip, and we couldn't
> take him home because Audrey would raise hell with him when
> he'd been drinking. So Jim Denny had told us the best thing to do
> in those cases was take him out there and let him dry out for a day
> or two.
>
> Hank'd say, "Where're we going, Shag?" and I'd say, "We'll be
> there in a minute, Hank." This was after we had gotten into town
> and dropped the other boys off. "Ain't we there yet?" he'd keep
> asking. I'd say, "We'll be there in just a minute." We'd pull up and
> I'd say, "O.K. Hank, we're here," and he'd raise up and look out
> and say, "Aw no, aw no, there's that damn Hut!" He didn't like to
> go there because they'd put him in the cottage and close the door.

He'd get sober there, though, because there wasn't nothing to drink.

We'd call and ask him, "What do you need, Hank?" and he'd say "Cigarettes, candy bars and funny books."

On about the second day, he'd be cold sober and he'd be bugging me, "When do you think *we're* going to get out of here?" and I'd say to myself, *Well, hell, I ain't in,* but I'd tell him, "I guess they'll probably let *us* out tomorrow."

People don't realize what you have to go through dealing with an alcoholic. After they sober up and come back, they're sorry and promise never to do it again — and they really mean it when they say it. Mother always wanted so much for Daddy, and I know she'd get awfully frustrated at times trying to deal with him.

The Big Book, the "bible" of Alcoholics Anonymous and the basic text for understanding and recovering from alcoholism, describes the wife's predicament:

We have travelled a rocky road, there is no mistake about that. We have had long rendezvous with hurt pride, frustration, self-pity, misunderstanding, and fear. These are not pleasant companions. We have been driven to maudlin sympathy, to bitter resentment.

Our loyalty and the desire that our husbands hold up their heads and be like other men have begotten all sorts of predicaments. We have been unselfish and self-sacrificing. We have told innumerable lies to protect our pride and our husbands' reputations. We have prayed, we have begged, we have been patient. We have struck out viciously. We have run away. We have been hysterical. We have been terror-stricken. We have sought sympathy. We have had retaliatory love affairs with other men.

Our homes have been battlegrounds many an evening. In the morning we have kissed and made up. Our friends have counseled chucking the men and we have done so with finality, only to be back in a little while hoping, always hoping. Our men have sworn great solemn oaths that they were through drinking forever. We have believed them when no one else could or would. Then, in days, weeks, or months, a fresh outburst.

Under these conditions, we naturally made mistakes. Some of them rose out of ignorance of alcoholism. Sometimes we sensed dimly that we were dealing with sick men. Had we fully understood the nature of the alcoholic illness, we might have behaved differently.

How could men who loved their wives and children be so unthinking, so callous, so cruel. There could be no love in such persons, we thought. And just as we were being convinced of their heartlessness, they would surprise us with fresh resolves and new attentions. For a while they would be their old sweet selves, only to dash the new structure of affection to pieces once more. Asked why they commenced drinking again, they would reply with some silly excuse, or none. It was so baffling, so heartbreaking.

It is now understood that a person cannot live with an active alcoholic without being profoundly affected themselves. As reality continues to be distorted, a couple in that situation will gradually lose touch with what a happy marital relationship is all about. That's what happened to Mother and Daddy. They turned against each other, and both began to blame the other for the failures in the marriage.

Those who work with alcoholics say that the wife of an alcoholic will eventually become resentful, uncommunicative, and out of control emotionally. Years of worry, false hope, confusion, and anger often make her turn over-protective, domineering, and possessive in her attempts to keep the lives of her husband and children in order. She may spend money obsessively, begin to drink herself, or adopt any of a number of addictive-type behavior patterns. She also becomes trapped in the role of victim and begins to question her own self-worth.

As success pressed harder on Daddy, his hunger increased for the simple pleasures of hunting and fishing and the rare peaceful moments they provided him. Jerry Rivers remembers many times when they performed their early morning radio shows in their hunting clothes with their guns propped against the studio wall, ready to "head for the woods at the last note of the closing theme."

Sometimes they hunted on some wooded farmland on Carter's Creek in Franklin, Tennessee. On September 1 Daddy purchased the farm for sixty thousand dollars from Mrs. Lois Brown, a widow. The 507-acre tract included an antebellum mansion, Beechwood Hall, built in 1856. It was situated on a hilltop, and you could see it from the entrance gate down on the road. It looked majestic, but Jerry Rivers remembers that the mansion was filled with bales of hay and needed a lot of work. It was a great source of pride to Daddy, and he hoped to fix up the house and move us out there to live.

One morning not long after Daddy bought the farm, he and Jerry were out there hunting when Daddy lost his balance jumping a ditch and fell into a rocky branch on his back. He was in severe pain, and Jerry rushed him home, where he was taken to the doctor.

Most people didn't know Daddy had a history of serious lower back problems. Some say they were due to a minor birth defect, "spina bifida occulta," or the slight herniation of several disks in his lower spine. I've heard that he was thrown from a horse as a teenager. That's when his back really started bothering him, and I know for a fact that he fell from the stage during his second Canadian tour in the spring. After the hunting accident, though, the severity of the pain he was experiencing meant that he could no longer avoid major surgery on his back. An operation was scheduled to be performed by Dr. Ben Fowler on December 13, 1951.

Daddy began to take "considerable medication" for his injury. This was very unfortunate, because an alcoholic, whose body is already tolerant to alcohol is instantly tolerant to sedatives and barbiturates, which also depress the central nervous system. This cross-tolerance, as it is called, speeds up the addiction process to the pain-killing drugs and further weakens the person's physical condition.

"Everyone wants to put Hank Williams in the drug scene," says Jerry, "but he didn't know what an illicit drug was. We'd warn him about the pills he was taking. We'd say, 'Hank, that stuff's got codeine and everything in the world in it. You don't want to take too many of those.' But he'd say, 'Well, it says take one every four hours. Think what four every hour'd do for you.' That was his reasoning."

Don Helms agrees. "He was just in a lot of pain, so he'd take whatever the doctor would give him to relieve his discomfort. He would use that back ailment to get to drink, though. We were driving down the road one time and he moaned, 'Ohh, my back.' I just kept on driving, and he said it again, 'Ohh, my back.' When I didn't stop and get him a drink, he kicked the back of my seat and said, 'Dammit, I said, "Oh, my back," and when I say "Oh my back" I mean "Oh my back!"'"

Daddy's physical pain was matched at times by his mental pain at being away from home so much. The great honky-tonk singer Lefty Frizzell worked with Daddy on tour occasionally and recalled, "he was lonesome being away from Audrey. He loved Audrey very much. I happened to be with him one time I think he talked to her for about an hour on the phone. He loved her dearly, and having to be out on a tour takes you away from home, and it made him blue."

✧ ✧ ✧ ✧ ✧

> The silence of a falling star lights up a purple sky,
> And as I wonder where you are,
> I'm so lonesome I could cry.

✧ ✧ ✧ ✧ ✧

When Daddy looked at Mother, he thought she was the prettiest thing he had ever seen. He knew she had a lot on the ball, and he was afraid that someone would come along and take her away from him.

They both were very jealous of each other. It's my belief that a lot of people in Nashville sort of helped make trouble between Mother and Daddy. Someone would tell one of them this and someone else would tell the other one that, and it created a lot of friction between them. I'm sure some people would have liked them to split up. As big a star as Daddy was, I'm sure there were other women who would have liked to see Daddy free.

✧ ✧ ✧ ✧ ✧

> If I didn't love you, I wouldn't be lonesome,
> And I'd never cry over you.
> If I didn't love you, I wouldn't be jealous.
> 'Cause I wouldn't care what you do.

✧ ✧ ✧ ✧ ✧

Daddy's success in 1951 should have been cause for great happiness and rejoicing for him and Mother, but instead the bottom began to drop out of their lives. You put together the years of drinking, their forced separations and jealousy, and the overwhelming strains of fame and lack of privacy — it was tearing their marriage apart.

Frances Preston, President of BMI, was working at WSM then and answered a lot of Daddy's fan mail. "Audrey tried very hard to be helpful to Hank," Frances says, "because she loved him, and he loved her. It was just an unfortunate situation where people get caught up in stardom, loneliness, and the times. You could see her at certain times really dressed well and wanting to be a lady, but that would be a night when perhaps he had had too much to drink. And then sometimes you could see him coming back in off the road, very tired and wanting to get home to his family, and he'd hear stories about things that she had been doing while he was gone. So they had a way of torturing each other."

❁   ❁   ❁   ❁   ❁

"I could tell the world you're doin' wrong,
That I was stringing you along,
And if that all were true,
I know I'd still want you."

❁   ❁   ❁   ❁   ❁

"Audrey was a lady," Mac McGee, the Corral's manager, insists. "She had morals. She was accused of a lot of things, but that doesn't make them so." McGee also claims that a lot of the "bums" that hung around the store caused trouble, exaggerating and distorting any occasion where Mother was seen with another man, no matter what the circumstances. As in the earlier days, this sort of troublemaker had something to gain in the way of a free party when Daddy got distraught over Mother.

I think Mother tried to protect Daddy by being a go-between whenever she could, but that only caused increased resentment toward her. On the other side, Mother had a hot temper. It got harder for her to control herself as Daddy got more jealous.

"If Audrey was out of his sight," remembers Dollie Denny, "he'd go crazy. I think it was just too much love, he couldn't cope with it. You've got to remember, Hank was just a kid.

Here he is, famous, and his wife is beautiful and classy and she's in the position of meeting all these people."

✿   ✿   ✿   ✿   ✿

I run around in circles
And turn in fire alarms.
I'm nutty as a fruitcake
When you're not in my arms.

CHAPTER 8

A House Without Love
Is Not a Home

I knew Mother and Daddy were fighting more when Daddy
was at home. One day Mother and I were riding down Franklin Road, going into town. Undoubtedly, they had just been in
an argument, because she said to me, "If it weren't for you and
Randall, I'd leave your daddy."

"What do you mean, you'd leave him?" I asked.

"I'd get a divorce."

I said, "Well, don't stay with him just because of me." I didn't
mean anything derogatory toward Daddy, but I didn't want it
to be my responsibility if she stayed with him when they were
unhappy. I don't think she was really unhappy, though. I think
she was mad.

Beside the time back in Montgomery when I came in on
Daddy spanking Mother, there was only one other occasion
when I saw him get upset enough to physically touch her. I
don't know what they were arguing about, but I was sitting in
the den watching TV when Mother came in and sat down and
Daddy followed her. They were kind of quiet for a little bit;
then they started. He looked over at me every once in a while,
and finally he said, "Don't you think it's time for her to go to
bed?" Mother said, "She's just fine right where she is." Of
course, she felt that he wouldn't do anything as long as I was in
the room.

He was trying to watch his language, but they started yell-ing, and it got pretty heated. Mother got up and started walking around, and she was cussing as bad as he was. All of a sudden, he just shoved her down in a chair that was behind her. He grabbed her shoulders and was going to shake her. When that happened, I jumped up and ran in between them. Of course, he quit immediately. He left the room, and I think he went out for a while. Mother said, "I think you better go on to bed now, Lycrecia." So I did.

Daddy was such a kind and gentle man by nature, but a lot of people saw that he could be violent when he was drinking. Zeke and Helen Clements, close friends of Mother and Daddy's since the Shreveport days, had moved to Nashville. They were frequent visitors at our home and were often called upon to mediate when things got out of hand. Helen recalls some of those times.

They were really having it. Audrey had followed my every step to keep Hank from being close to her. When she had to go to the bathroom, he got between us and went in and locked the door.

I said, "Hank, open this door. What are you doing in there?"

He said, "It's all right, Helen, I just slapped her so she'd stop and listen to me. That's all I done."

Audrey could say some pretty ugly things, and then she'd start crying and that would really set him off.

I wasn't afraid till he had a gun. I said, "Audrey, I don't like this."

She said, "He won't hurt you, he likes you."

I had to sleep with her in her room with the door locked and make Hank a bed in the den. When he started waving the gun around, I said, "Audrey, I'm getting out of here. You can stay if you want, but he's violent." I said to Hank, "You don't want to do this," but he wasn't listening. I started out the back door, and she was right behind me. We went next door. That was the only time I saw him with a gun.

One night we were coming back from the Opry. We had picked Hank up and they got into a fuss, and she made him get out of the car. He said he'd walk home. I made her go back and get him. I said, "Audrey, you're not going to leave him out there on the side of the road like that."

She said, "Well, I am, too. I'm not going back." Finally she did, though.

Another night he came home and got mad and was leaving. I

told Audrey, "He'll be back after a while; he's not going nowhere far." She was crying because they'd been fussing, and she didn't believe me.

Hank said, "I'll call a cab and go out to the airport."

I said, "Hank, let me drive you."

He said, "No, you stay here. I'm going to just wait outside for the cab. You can come out there and talk to me while I wait if you want." When we got outside, he put a whole bunch of bills — about five hundred-dollar bills — in my hand and said, "Give these to her, but don't do it until I've left."

I went in and gave them to her and she said, "I don't want them."

I said, "Well, what do you want me to do with them, Audrey?"

She said, "I don't care what you do with them. You can keep them, you can tear them up, but I just don't care!"

His drinking bothered Audrey bad. She would find bottles he had hidden in the house, and she'd pour them down the sink. One time she was cranky, and she said, "Let him drink all he wants," and she went and got him three fifths. He was already so drunk he couldn't get off the couch, but he drank it all and we had to take him to the hospital.

There were peaceful times, though. We'd have fun. One time Hank said, "I just wrote this song, Helen, and I want you to listen to it and tell me what you think."

I said, "I don't know, Hank."

He said, "No, really, just tell me what you honestly think." He played the thing and asked, "Well, what do you think?"

"I think it stinks," I said.

"Well, hell," he said, "what do you know about music anyhow."

Zeke continues, "Hank'd complain about how much money she spent on clothes, and I'd say, 'You can see where she spent it at least.' But then he'd turn around and give her whatever she wanted. In spite of it all, though, she really loved Hank, and he really loved her. He'd tell me, 'When I'm out on the road and I start toward Nashville, I think about Audrey and my passion rises.'

"Then one time we were fishing at Old Kentucky Lake, and he was telling me his troubles. I said, 'Well, Hank, you've tried everything else. Have you ever thought of trying religion?' He answered, 'No, because I'm afraid to.' I never was really sure what he meant by that."

Daddy had always been fascinated by guns. As a small boy in Georgiana, he had the nickname "two-gun Pete" because he loved to dress up and play in cowboy gear. Also, by necessity, he always packed a variety of weapons during his early career as an entertainer on the "blood bucket" circuit of roadside clubs throughout the rural South.

Guns were just a part of everyday life in the area where Daddy grew up. Many men still relied on their hunting skills to put meat on the family table, and they did not wait for hunting season to practice their favorite sport.

Jerry Rivers writes on this subject: "Hank Williams' admiration for old guns, particularly pistols, was almost uncontrollable. He would usually become acquainted with local policemen, sheriffs, and deputies wherever we worked, and they would help him locate and buy guns that he wanted."

Grant Turner could never understand Daddy's attachment to his guns. "Hank felt like he had to have a gun around, but then he'd hide it. A fella who worked at a service station on Franklin Road took care of a gun for him. I heard Hank used to leave the gun with this fella before he went home. I don't know whether he felt like he needed it for protection or what it was, but he carried that gun with him when he went out in the evening."

June Carter Cash, daughter of Mother Maybelle of the original Carter family and wife of Johnny Cash, knew Mother and Daddy during this bleak period of late 1951. She recounts once when her sister Anita was driving Mother's car and Daddy tried to run her off the road, thinking it was Mother. June says the entire Carter family was afraid of what Daddy might do because of his inability to eat or sleep.

"Dammit I love her," Hank cursed.

"It was a love with such possession, power, jealousy, and hate," explains June, "that it consumed like a fire. It was burning him alive."

                ❂   ❂   ❂   ❂   ❂

> You have no heart, you have no shame,
> You take true love and give the blame.
> I guess that I should not complain,
> I love you still, you win again."

                ❂   ❂   ❂   ❂   ❂

Miss Ragland says Daddy once complained to her that "Audrey can turn her love on and off like you do a faucet, but I can't do that." She recalls that "when he got drunk, he was pretty mean, all right. Most of the time, though, he'd call her and she'd know he was drunk. She'd take me and the kids, and we'd get away from the house. Even when Mrs. Williams couldn't get us all out, I'd try to get Lycrecia and Randall out of it as much as I could. A lot of times we went over to the Harlans next door and played out in their yard until things got smoothed over. Things began to get a little rough, and then they got a little rougher and a little rougher. But I didn't feel bad about Mr. Williams and neither did Lycrecia. He was a good man; it was just his drinking."

Mother's sister Lynette can just picture Daddy tugging off his boots and telling Mother she always wanted to change him. Then again, Lynette recalls another time when "Lycrecia and I got in the bathroom at one end of the house because they were carrying on so bad at the other end. Finally, Lycrecia got so upset that she left and went down to the barn."

Daddy's back surgery was on December 13, 1951, at Vanderbilt Hospital. It was considered a medical success, but his recovery got off to a bad start. He convinced the hospital staff to let him out a few days early so he could be home before Christmas. Mother fussed with him for leaving early, and, according to Wesley Rose, Daddy got angry and threw a chair and had to go back to the hospital again.

The doctors had told Daddy not to get up without his metal back brace except to go to the bathroom and back to bed. So Daddy just stayed in the bed. Every once in awhile he'd put it on, but usually he'd go into the kitchen and sit at the table a little bit. Then he'd go back to bed because his back would start hurting.

On Christmas Eve, Mother asked me — I was ten and a half and didn't believe in Santa Claus anymore — "Lycrecia, since your Daddy is in bed and he can't go up and down the stairs, do you want to help me get Hank, Jr.'s stuff from Santa Claus down from the attic?" Well, it tickled me to death to be a part of that.

We went back into the bedroom where Daddy was, and Mother said "We're going upstairs to the attic, and Lycrecia's going to help me get the Christmas presents since you can't get up and down the stairs right now."

Now Daddy was a very sentimental person. Mother was more practical, and this conversation really irritated him. I think it hurt him that I was growing up and didn't believe in Santa Claus anymore. He still wanted to play Santa Claus for both of his kids.

He said, "You mean to tell me you're going to let her help get stuff down that Santa Claus is bringing?"

"Well, Honey," Mother said, "she knows there's not a Santa Claus anymore, and I need some help and you can't help me right now."

Daddy had a fit. He really was mad. He got up out of the bed and came to the doorway in the kitchen as we were pulling the ladder down to go upstairs. Then he came into the kitchen, and he was cussing and Mother was cussing back at him. I began to wish Mother hadn't even asked me to help her.

Mother was trying to keep things under control because she knew Daddy was not feeling very well, so she left the room. But Daddy got up and followed her out of the kitchen. Finally Daddy went back to bed. I think he hurt his back while he was up. I remember Mother and I went on upstairs and got the presents down for Hank, Jr.

I didn't hear anything else out of him, and I went to bed not too long after that. That was the last of the argument I heard, but they must have kept it going.

Later that night, Mother called Mr. Harlan next door and told him she wished he would come over and see about Hank. He was in a "terribly foul mood" and had been waving a gun around. "So I walked around the house and peeked in the window," recalls Mr. Harlan, "and I saw him there. I felt so sorry for him. He looked so lonely. I went to the door to tell Hank who I was, and he said to come in. He was in such pain, and he was so lonely. I said, 'Let me go over to my house and get you some eggnog.' He said, 'I'd love it. I might put a little stuff in it.' I said, 'Fine. Do you have any, or do you want me to bring some?' He said, 'I have it.' I'm glad I went over there. I stayed over an hour talking to him. I treasured his friendship. Audrey came back sometime that night."

❋   ❋   ❋   ❋   ❋

Why don't you spark me like you used to do,
And say sweet nothins' like you used to coo,
I'm the same old trouble that you've always been through,
So why don't you love me like you used to do?

❋   ❋   ❋   ❋   ❋

Lynette came up to stay with us the week between Christmas and New Year's. Being several years older than I was and
less emotionally involved, she was able to see that the situation
between Mother and Daddy was extremely serious. Lynette
remembers the week well.

I can remember that Hank talked about the pain being something
fierce, and he didn't understand why he should be having so much
pain after the operation.

While I was there, they had an argument and Audrey left. Miss
Ragland was off that week, and I took care of Hank, Jr. Audrey
had driven off somewhere in the car, and she didn't come back
until sometime that night because I rocked Hank, Jr., to sleep that
night. Hank, Sr., was up and walking around because I remember
well sitting there rocking the baby, and Hank, Sr., would come in
and pat him on the back and rub his head. Hank, Jr., was crying,
and we couldn't get him quieted down.

That night, Daddy [Mr. Sheppard] rode the bus up from home,
and he had the driver stop right there in front of the house as it
went by on the way downtown to the station. I remember that
Hank, Sr., went to the door — he was surprised to see Daddy and
I was, too. I don't know if he had come to see Hank or if he knew
that things were not too good, or maybe he had just come to take
me home. But he wanted to know where Audrey was, and Hank
told him they had words and she got into the car and drove off.

Daddy was scheduled to appear in Baltimore in a New Year's
Eve show with Lefty Frizzell and Peewee King, but the date
had been set before his operation. Now his doctors would not
let him go. He was disappointed and depressed, so he recorded
a statement of apology and explanation to his fans.

Well, howdy friends. This is Hank Williams. Hope all you folks
are enjoying yourselves here at the show in Baltimore today. I'm

awful sorry that I can't be with you today. I'd like to say thanks to
my very good friend Jimmie Davis for pinch-hitting for me today.
Also my boys, they're all here, and my wife, Audrey.

On December the thirteenth, I had to have an operation that
I've been putting off for about a year. I had to have it because I'd
finally got to where I couldn't even walk on one leg hardly. So at
the time I had it, I thought I could make this date here in Baltimore. But when he started the operation, when the doctor got
into my back, he found a lot wrong that he hadn't anticipated
before, so naturally he had to go ahead and fix it all. I had what
you call a spine fusion, I had two ruptured disks in my back. The
first and second vetebrae was no good, it was just deformed or
broken when I was a child or wore out or something. He said he
thought I'd rode a few too many hundred thousand miles in these
automobiles. So he went ahead and fixed it so after I came to . . .
he told me it'd be impossible for me to be out of here before the
first of February.

So then me and Mr. Denny at the station here, we tried to talk
him into letting me take an airplane with a stretcher in it, an ambulance, fly up to Washington and take an ambulance from there
over to Baltimore. But he wouldn't go along with it, so he just
finally said no. He says, "You're gonna have to stay at home." So
that just means that I won't be there, but I'd like to say thanks to
you people for buying my records, requesting the songs.

I knew about this date before the operation, and I fully intended to be in there, but that's just one of those things that happened that you can't get by. So I know you're going to have a good
time with Peewee King, Lefty Frizzell, all my boys, and Audrey,
and my very good friend, Jimmie Davis. I'd like to promise you as
soon as I get out of this bed, I figure on coming to Baltimore and
making a personal appearance. And I sure wisht I could swap this
bed today for the stage in Baltimore. Until I see you again, thank
you a lot, and I know you'll have a good time. Bye now.

When it became clear to Jim Denny that Daddy would not
be able to make the Baltimore show, he and Mother agreed
that she would make an appearance herself in Baltimore to
assure the audience that Daddy was truly ill and not intoxicated. She went and personally delivered Daddy's recorded
message, but it was not easy for her to get away from
Nashville. She has written about that New Year's Eve.

Hank started acting up before I left to go do this date, so I took the children and left. We stayed at the home of Mr. and Mrs. Garrett, the couple who had sold us Lycrecia's pony.

I hadn't taken many clothes with me, though, so I went back home to pack some things for the trip to Baltimore. Three elderly women whose husbands were Nashville businessmen came with me. I knew he was acting up, but I was just hoping I could slip in and out and get some clothes and go on.

So we were just easing around — I knew he was very edgy — and as I walked out the door, a gun shot four times. I could hardly walk. I thought the woman who was driving me would never get the car started because she was completely scared to death.

I don't think Hank was really shooting at me. I don't really know if he wanted me to think that or if he wanted me to think he was shooting himself. I went on to Baltimore anyway. New Year's Eve night I called him, and I said, "Hank, I'll never live with you another day." And a year to the day from that night is when he passed away.

Hank, Jr., and I stayed with the Garretts, and Ray Garrett drove Mother to the airport New Year's Eve morning to catch the plane to Washington, D.C., just outside of Baltimore. Miss Ragland had returned from her Christmas holiday and answered Mother's call that night. She handed the phone over to Daddy when she realized the nature of the call.

✧ ✧ ✧ ✧ ✧

The simple things have gone forever
We wanted wealth to call our own.
And now we've reached the hour of parting,
A house without love is not a home.

CHAPTER 9

And the Last Word Led
to a Divorce

One day something happened,
It was nothing, of course,
But one word led to another,
And the last word led to a divorce.

❀   ❀   ❀   ❀   ❀

By January 3 Daddy had moved out of the house and into
the Andrew Jackson Hotel in downtown Nashville. Don
Helms visited him there, and Daddy told him, "I don't think I
can go back this time."

When Mother returned home from Baltimore, she called
Daddy's cousin Marie Harvell and told her about the separation. Marie and Louis King, a detective in Montgomery and a
good friend of Daddy's, came to Nashville to take him back to
Montgomery to complete his recuperation from his recent surgery at his mother's boardinghouse. He stayed in Montgomery
a couple of weeks, but he returned to Nashville sometime later
in January.

He moved into a house at the corner of Natchez Trace and
Westwood Drive that was already being rented by Ray Price.
Daddy settled into a six-month siege of parties, drinking,
painkillers, and sleeplessness. During this period, Daddy
didn't take care of himself. He was depressed, and he would
drink to forget about his problems with Mother. His back hurt,

---

but he wouldn't use the cane or brace, so then he took the painkillers. Well, painkillers and alcohol do not mix.

His first time back on the stage after his surgery, on January 29 and 30 at the Mosque in Richmond, Virginia, was a disaster. Ray Price appeared with him and practically had to carry the two shows on the twenty-ninth because Daddy was too sick and drunk to handle them himself. The crowds were restless and angry; many of them tried to get their money back. A reviewer for the Richmond *Times-Dispatch*, Edith Lindeman, wrote a critical piece about Daddy after the first show, but Daddy opened the show the next night by dedicating his number, "Mind Your Own Business," to her.

In the meantime, on January 10 Mother had filed her bill of complaint and writs of injunction against Daddy's assets in the first stage of the divorce procedure. Along with Daddy, she named as defendants Acuff-Rose, WSM, Loew's, Inc. (which owned MGM Record Division), First American Bank, and Third National Bank. They were the holders, in one form or another, of Daddy's assets: the home on Franklin Road and its furnishings, three Cadillacs, the farm on Carter's Creek and livestock, the Corral, bank accounts, song and record royalties, and personal and radio appearance income.

In the complaint Mother filed, she recalled the:

cruel and inhuman treatment which had been inflicted upon the complainant by defendant at numerous times, and practically throughout their entire married life, the degree and extent thereof having become more intense within the last several months, to the point that even though complainant has every desire to maintain the home of the parties, and to preserve this marriage, she is not physically or mentally able further to endure this mistreatment.

Defendant is a man of violent disposition when aroused [the document continued] and this violence is particularly aggravated when the complainant, herself, is the object thereof.

Writs of injunction were requested against Acuff-Rose, WSM, and Loew's to prevent them from paying Daddy more than one-half of "any amounts owing to him" and against Daddy himself, to keep him "from coming about, interfering with, or molesting complainant, Audrey Mae Williams, at any place, either in public or in private, at her home, on the streets, at the store known as 'Hank and Audrey's Corral,' or elsewhere."

Along with these preliminary requests, Mother included her petition to be awarded custody of Hank, Jr. My custody was not mentioned because I had never been legally adopted. Daddy had always hoped to be my legal father, but Mother told me later that she wouldn't let him adopt me because she was afraid that he would take me away from her if they ever divorced. Mother and Daddy had had so many marriage problems.

Daddy did not file his response until March, at which time he took the opportunity to present his version of their marital problems and who was to blame. He denied that he had been "guilty of any act of cruel or inhuman treatment or conduct towards the complainant as would render it unsafe and improper for them to live together . . . . But, on the contrary, he [would] show to the court upon the hearing that he [had] suffered every humiliation, abuse, and mistreatment that a man could possibly take from a woman at the hands of the complainant in this cause . . ."

Then Daddy made his own accusations. His complaint stated that from early on in their marriage:

> the cross-defendant refused to appreciate the obligations of married life, denying her attentions and affections to her home and husband, insisting that she, too, was an entertainer and singer of ability . . . with the result that she steadfastly refused to keep house or maintain the home as a mother and wife, but insisted on leaving the children with others and accompanying your cross-complainant on the road.

> Even this far back the cross-defendant, who has always been possessed of an ungovernable temper, would fly into fits and rages and curse and abuse, and condemn and castigate your cross-complainant, both privately and in the presence of others, because she could not share the program with him. However, your cross-complainant, while denied the comforts and assurances of a solid and substantial home life by reasons of the cross-defendant's appetite for public appearances and her consequent neglect of their home and children, kept pushing and plugging ahead trying to better their conditions and exploit his abilities as much as possible.

Daddy complained of mother's extravagances and "notwith-standing the fact that she was furnished with every convenience and luxury that money could buy . . . has always insisted upon traveling about, acting independent . . . seeking and having everything she wanted and a good time all the time."

He did admit, however, "that he has sought to buy her interest," although he said she had never shown any appreciation for that fact. He accused her of flying into rages of temper and fits and throwing "furniture and articles" at him.

The document took a rough turn as he described her "carousing around both during the daytime and nighttime, both in Nashville and in Davidson County, and in other counties and states with other men."

He recounted how, "on innumerable occasions [she] told him that she did not love him, that she hated him, and that she didn't expect to live with him." Then, in a sad and revealing paragraph, he claimed that "about eighteen months ago, the cross-defendant became pregnant, and this made the cross-complainant very happy. . . . However, much to his humiliation and grief, he learned later that the cross-defendant had had an abortion performed on her in her home, and had become infected and had to be carried to St. Thomas Hospital." Miss Ragland recently verified this information that had been kept private for many years.

"There is now not any chance for them to ever live together in peace and happiness," Daddy stated. He concluded by suing for divorce on his own grounds and requesting to be granted custody of Hank, Jr., since "cross-defendant has been guilty of such misconduct that it is impossible to even think about her rearing the child."

I can read these accusations and see that Mother and Daddy each had some degree of truth in their charges against the other, and they each had blind hurt and rage. Neither one of them mentioned alcohol or drunkenness in their petitions, although for anyone who knew them personally, the drinking and its consequences could be read between all the lines.

The settlement, dated April 3, stated that the parties could make no agreement as to a divorce but had drawn up the property and custody agreement in the event a divorce was granted.

In such case, Mother would retain custody of Hank, Jr., would be granted full title to the Franklin Road house, including furnishings, would keep her yellow Cadillac convertible, and would get half of all Daddy's royalties as long as she did not remarry.

According to numerous sources, including Daddy's cousin Marie and Ray Price, the terms of the final property and custody settlement with Mother represented Daddy's own wishes. I think he loved Mother enough that he didn't want her to go without anything. I also think he hoped that they might get back together again. He really didn't want the divorce, but he had always let her have her way, and she said that was what she wanted so he went through with it.

Daddy received full title to their Western wear clothing business (which he sold to Mac McGee in June 1952), the farm in Franklin, Tennessee (which he sold in September 1952), and his other cars.

The final divorce decree, including the custody and property settlement of April 3, was granted on May 29, 1952. The court found Mother's allegations in her original bill to be sustained by proof, that "the defendant, Hank Williams, has been guilty of such cruel and inhuman treatment or conduct toward the complainant, Audrey Mae Williams, as renders cohabitation unsafe and improper, and renders it unsafe and improper for her to be under his dominion and control."

The court "ordered, adjudged, and decreed" that "the complainant, Audrey Mae Williams, be and she hereby is granted an absolute divorce from the defendant, Hank Williams, forever dissolving the bonds of matrimony heretofore subsisting between them, and restoring to her all the rights and privileges of an unmarried person."

It was entered on the court records, but it would never penetrate the hearts of Mother or Daddy. Neither would ever be free of their love for each other.

❉   ❉   ❉   ❉   ❉

It's hard to know another's lips will kiss you,
And hold you just the way I used to do.
Oh heaven only knows how much I miss you,
I can't help it if I'm still in love with you.

CHAPTER 10

I Don't Care If Tomorrow Never Comes

When Mother and Daddy divorced, I sort of placed myself in a vacuum. I just went about my everyday routines. I laughed and had a good time, and I just wouldn't think about unpleasant things. I don't remember feeling angry at Daddy. I missed him when he never came back to the house, but I just didn't dwell on it. I've thought many times that if I had been an older child, I would have been able to understand better and talk it over with them. Maybe I could even have helped them because I know they regretted it later that their tempers had gotten the better of them.

✧   ✧   ✧   ✧   ✧

> We had our love to make us happy,
> It wasn't meant to bring us tears,
> Love like ours should never die,
> So, Darling, let's turn back the years.

✧   ✧   ✧   ✧   ✧

If Mother and Daddy would have had access to the modern books on the disease of alcoholism, they would have found the story of the next year written on many of the pages. Experts say that when someone leaves an alcoholic spouse he or she is leaving a sick and dying person. There is no way that walking out can aid in the alcoholic's recovery. Rather than having a shock effect, it usually causes the alcoholic to drink even more to erase the memory of an "untrue" love. Often, following a divorce, the alcoholic winds up in a hospital or on the death-bed. Resentful and bitter, he feels completely forsaken and desperate and his drinking becomes heavier than ever before.

An old Japanese proverb tells the whole story of the alcoholic process: "First, man takes a drink. Then the drink takes a drink. Then the drink takes the man." This was certainly true with Mother and Daddy.

Miss Ragland recalls that Mother was upset after the separation but tried to hide it. "Mrs. Williams tried to pretend she was so happy she didn't know what to do, but I knew that down deep in her heart she was hurting. But that's the way she was. She didn't want people to know her real feelings. To tell the truth about it, I was afraid at times they was going to kill each other. I knew that they loved each other, but they had too much water under the bridge."

Helen Clements believes that Mother never really wanted the divorce.

> I think it was just one of those things she just got caught up in, always talking divorce, divorce. They were both so stubborn, neither one of them would make the first move. They had just talked about it until it was a decision, and neither one knew how to get out of it.
>
> People thought she didn't care anything for Hank, but I knew different. One afternoon we went to a movie and when we came out, Audrey looked at the time and she said, "Oh, Hank will be at the hotel for about an hour and a half. I'm going to call him." And she did.

Mother stepped up her activities, social and professional, to occupy her thoughts and her time. She planned some personal appearance tours of her own. The *Billboard* of May 17, 1952, announced that "Jeri Carr and her all-girl band have signed to do a series of one-nighters with Audrey Williams' troupe."

I only saw Daddy a few times after he and Mother separated. On Mother's Day he took me and Hank, Jr., and Miss Ragland over to the house on Natchez Trace that he shared with Ray Price and showed us his gun collection. I don't remember him having that many guns over at our home. If he had them, he must have kept them out of my sight.

It was during this time that Daddy began to date a Nashville secretary named Bobbie Jett. He had heard that Mother seemed to be enjoying her freedom, so he was determined that he would, too. Bobbie Jett became a regular visitor to the Natchez Trace house, and by early April she discovered that she was pregnant.

Daddy's cousin Marie began to make more frequent trips to Nashville after he and Mother separated.

Audrey would call me and say, "Marie, I think you need to come to Nashville." She cared about Hank and kept up on how he was doing. I'd catch the first train out of Montgomery and go over to the house where he was living with Ray Price.

Once Audrey came over there and wanted to talk to Bobbie. I said she wasn't there, and Audrey said, "Marie, don't tell me that. I'm going to sit right here with you all night long, but I'm going to see her." So I told Bobbie, and she came out and talked to Audrey. I don't know what they talked about, but they were friendly to each other.

To look at what Daddy did during the first half of 1952, you might not think his grip on the world was slipping with each passing day. On March 26 he sang "Hey Good-Lookin'" on the first half hour of the "Kate Smith Show" out of New York City. The kinescope from this show is the only known surviving video record of a Hank Williams performance. There was a tremendous response to his appearance, and on April 9 he did a second spot on the popular network show.

Minnie Pearl was booked on a show with Daddy in San Diego in late April. She recalls that he was in terrible shape from his drinking and the pills he was taking to ease the pain in his back. "When he saw me he said, 'Oh Minnie!' and he started to cry. It was a dreadful occasion for me because I loved Hank."

Minnie tried to convince the promoter who was handling the tour that Daddy was too sick to work. They put him on the stage anyway, but he was not able to perform and the audience grew impatient.

"So the promoter told me to take him and stay in the car with him until the next show and keep him away from anything to drink or take. They put him in the front seat of the car with the promoter's wife, and I sat in the back seat. Someone else was back there with me, but I can't remember who it was. I kept trying to talk to him, but he was like a caged animal. We were driving around San Diego, and he was so nervous and restless that I said, 'Let's sing.' He started singing 'I Saw The Light' and we all started singing. Then he stopped us, and he said, 'I don't want to sing that song because there ain't no light, Minnie; there ain't no light.'"

From April 29 through May 2, Daddy was part of an Opry package show that also included Carl Smith, Ernest Tubb, the Carter Family, the Duke of Paducah, Lew Childre, and Annie Lou and Danny. They played benefit shows to sellout crowds in Beaumont, Corpus Christi, and Houston. Daddy's band members had begun to take other jobs, and the Drifting Cowboys did not accompany him to Texas.

Daddy and his Drifting Cowboys were scheduled to work at the Last Frontier Club in Las Vegas, Nevada, the last two weeks in May. Jerry Rivers and Don Helms drove him out there. Jim Denny sent along an ex-policeman named Charlie Sanders to keep tabs on Daddy during the two-week engagement. Daddy arrived in Las Vegas drunk, however, and, as things got worse, the club management decided to cancel the contract after only five days.

Dollie Denny calls the Las Vegas affair "the straw that broke the camel's back" in regard to Daddy's being a reliable performer. In one instance, Daddy was locked in his room, but he tied his boots to a bedsheet and lowered them. A bellboy filled them with bottles of liquor, which Daddy then reeled back up. When Charlie Sanders opened the door to check in on Daddy, he was surprised to find him definitely drunk.

Danny Dill, who was part of the show there, claims that "Hank blew it deliberately. There's no other way you can say it. He was one of the first hillbilly singers to go to Las Vegas, and after that he was supposed to go to California to be in a movie. I think the man was scared. Hank was a genius. But he began to see that he was becoming a thing, a salable product, and he didn't know how to handle it. 'They're slicing me up and selling me like baloney,' he complained to me."

       ◊   ◊   ◊   ◊   ◊

I don't care if tomorrow never comes,
This world holds nothing for me.
I've been lonely night and day ever since you went away,
So I don't care if tomorrow never comes.

       ◊   ◊   ◊   ◊   ◊

During the early summer months, Daddy did manage to complete a tour of Indiana and Illinois and then do two recording sessions in Nashville. In the first session, on June 13, he sang "Window Shopping," "Jambalaya," "Settin' The Woods On Fire," and "I'll Never Get Out Of This World Alive." On July 11 he recorded two jukebox tunes, "You Win Again" and "I Won't Be Home No More," and two as Luke the Drifter: "Be Careful Of Stones That You Throw" and "Why Don't You Make Up Your Mind."

The Saturday night Opry was Daddy's only real obligation ever since his surgery and separation from Mother, but his drinking and unpredictable behavior had created a set of problems for the people who ran the Opry. His popularity was at an all-time high, but the honorable reputation of the "Grand Ole Opry" was at stake every time he missed a show or appeared drunk on the stage. Finally, on August 11, 1952, Jim Denny called him and told him by phone that he was fired because he had not made the "Friday Night Frolics" after being warned that he would be in serious trouble if he missed it.

Johnnie Wright was at the house on Natchez Trace with Daddy when he received the call. "You can't fire me, I've already quit!" was Daddy's reply.

"Hank was drinking real bad," remembers Johnny. "I was over there on Natchez Trace with him a lot then. He leaned against the screen door one time — he thought it was latched — and fell out the door and skinned his face all up.

"'It just busted my heart when she left me. It's really hard to take.' That's the words he said to me."

✿   ✿   ✿   ✿   ✿

It's hard to know you'll never have
The one you love so true.
While the world's asleep, I'll lay and cry
I lost the only love I knew.

✿   ✿   ✿   ✿   ✿

Johnnie helped Daddy load up his few possessions and drove him down to the National Life Building to pick up his last check. Daddy did not go in because he was really weak from all the drinking he had been doing and was stretched out on a recliner in the back of Johnnie's limousine. Then Johnnie and his brother-in-law drove Daddy to his mother's boardinghouse in Montgomery. "When Hank was leaving town," says Don Helms, "I went to see him to give him some stuff that belonged to him, and when I got home I told my wife he wouldn't live another six months."

Daddy managed to pull himself together for the Hank Williams Homecoming Day on August 15 in Greenville, Alabama. He rode in the parade that day in a new blue Cadillac convertible that he had bought just before leaving Nashville. "He had two cars," says Marie. "One was the color of Audrey's hair, and then he bought one the color of her eyes."

✿   ✿   ✿   ✿   ✿

Golden hair and big blue eyes,
She could win a beauty prize,
There's nothin' as sweet as my baby.

✿   ✿   ✿   ✿   ✿

I think Daddy bought that convertible because Mother always drove a convertible. After they divorced, he wanted to show her that he wasn't married anymore, so he could have a convertible, too.

From Greenville, Mrs. Stone had arranged for Daddy to have a week's vacation out on Lake Martin, about thirty miles from Montgomery. His friend, a radio disk jockey named Bob McKinnon, rented his cousin's cabin for Daddy and Bobbie Jett, who was about five months pregnant by then.

Lake Martin covered the site of the old Creek Indian town

of Kowliga, and Daddy composed most of his classic song "Kaw-Liga" about the lovesick wooden Indian there at the lake cabin. He also put the finishing touches on "Your Cheatin' Heart." At the end of the week, Fred Rose flew down to meet Daddy in Montgomery and added the humorous refrain to "Kaw-Liga."

During that same week, on August 17, Daddy was arrested and jailed in Alexander City for being drunk and disorderly. He was hallucinating from the DT's (delirium tremens) that afflict advanced alcoholics, and he stayed in jail until Bob McKinnon came down and paid his bail. The police chief Winfred Patterson remembers Daddy saying that he'd been in "worse jails and some better." A photo taken at the time of his arrest shows a sick and forlorn young man.

By the end of August, Jo Stafford's record of "Jambalaya" had hit the best-selling charts, *Billboard* carried an article recognizing him as a leader in the pop field. It reported that Daddy's thirty-one singles released by MGM over the course of their five-year association had sold more than ten million records to date.

Somehow Daddy continued to work. He played to a record crowd on his twenty-ninth birthday in San Antonio. On September 20 he appeared on the "Louisiana Hayride" for the first time in nearly three years. Then, on September 23 he was in Nashville for what was to be the last recording session of his life. "I Could Never Be Ashamed of You," "Your Cheatin' Heart," "Kaw-Liga," and "Take These Chains from My Heart" were recorded that afternoon.

During September and October he played in Missouri, Texas, Oklahoma, Kansas, and Louisiana. At the Baton Rouge High School auditorium in early October, he ran into his old friend Lum York, who was then working with Lefty Frizzell. "I went down there that night to the auditorium," says Lum, "and he asked me did I want to play the show with him and I told him, 'Yeah.' The doctor had given him something to take and had told him, 'Now when you take this, do you want to die?' Hank said, 'No' and the doctor said, 'Well, if you take anything to drink while you're taking this stuff, it'll kill you deader than a hammer.'"

As Daddy was reaching out for some kind of help in his final days, he met a "Dr." Toby Marshall during the fall of 1952 in Oklahoma City. When Daddy had been unable to work one night there, Marshall had appeared to give him a shot that immediately sobered him up and allowed him to perform. The use of sedatives and barbiturates was an experimental method of treating alcoholism in those days. Actually, this only speeded up the addictive process and caused severe physical side effects.

Mother had always been Daddy's protector from the hangers-on that surround all successful entertainers. She had sacrificed her own popularity among Daddy's friends many times over the years in order to shelter him from the users that he attracted like a magnet.

Now it was Lillie Stone's job to keep track of everything, to make sure Daddy was sober when he needed to be, to rescue him from untrustworthy characters and awkward situations, and, generally, to run all of his affairs. This was a role she had filled a number of years earlier, but it was many times more complicated and hopeless now. When Toby Marshall promised her to keep Daddy straight, she must have thought she had stumbled onto a miracle.

Marshall became a fairly constant companion to Daddy, supplying him with an endless assortment of prescription medications, including the highly addictive painkiller morphine and chloral hydrate, a hypnotic sedative used to bring on deep sleep. Whether or not Toby Marshall prescribed the anti-buse, the treatment for alcoholism that, combined with a drink, could cause death, is unknown. No one found out until much later that Marshall was a "self-styled doctor" as well as an ex-convict on parole in Oklahoma for a forgery conviction.

Daddy began to appear at hospitals and sanitariums through the fall and winter of 1952, following the exact course of alcoholism as described in the Alcoholics Anonymous *Big Book*. His body, especially his heart, began to show the ravages of the alcohol and prescription drugs. He suffered at least two minor heart attacks, and his face and body were sometimes swollen and bloated. He thought he was getting fat, says his cousin Marie, and the doctors told his family to go along with his belief that he was gaining weight to avoid upsetting him.

＊　＊　＊　＊　＊

I don't care if tomorrow never comes,
This world holds nothing for me.
I've been lonely night and day since you went away,
So I don't care if tomorrow never comes.

＊　＊　＊　＊　＊

On October 18, 1952, less than three months before his death, Daddy married Billie Jean Jones Eshliman, a nineteen-year-old redheaded beauty from Bossier City, Louisiana. The next day they repeated the ceremony during two shows on the stage of the Municipal Auditorium in New Orleans.

Even at my age, I heard the talk about Daddy marrying Billie Jean. I never did meet her, though, because they weren't together very long. Daddy was in such bad shape then. He was drunk almost all the time and literally nothing but skin and bones. He even called Mother and invited her to come to the wedding, telling her he would send her a ticket down there if she wanted to come. Of course, she didn't go. I know Daddy married Billie Jean just to spite Mother.

June Carter Cash, who was married to singer Carl Smith at the time, wrote in her autobiographical book *From the Heart,* that she and Carl and Daddy were at a baseball game one day not long before he married Billie Jean when he saw a woman he thought was Audrey.

"He could always see her somewhere," June noted.

June's sister Anita was getting married and Daddy said that he was getting married, too. "I wish it was Audrey," he said.

Two days after Daddy and Billie Jean filed for their marriage license and three days before they actually married, Daddy was in Montgomery, signing an unusual agreement with Bobbie Jett regarding the child she was due to deliver "on or about the first day of January 1953." Bobbie had been living in Mrs. Stone's boardinghouse since she had followed Daddy out of Nashville in mid-August and accompanied him to Lake Martin.

Although Daddy would only admit that he "may be the father of said child," the document specified a number of arrangements agreed upon by the parties. He was to pay his mother for Bobbie's room and board from that date, October

15, until January 15, 1953. He was to pay all doctor and hospital bills in connection with the birth and also a monthly allowance of one hundred dollars (plus two hundred dollars in cash for "immediate and necessary expenses"). These payments were to be disbursed by Mrs. Stone. Bobbie Jett would be paid, additionally, one hundred dollars a month following the birth of the baby. Then, "within thirty days after the birth of said child, the said Hank Williams shall provide a one-way plane ticket to the said Bobbie W. Jett from Montgomery to any place in California which she may designate" and the child would be placed in Lillie Stone's custody "for a period of two years after its birth," with Daddy providing all necessary financial support.

The last item in the document adds a twist in light of all that has happened since Daddy signed it: "In view of the fact that the paternity of said child is in doubt and is not to be in any way construed as admitted by this agreement which is made solely because of the possibility of paternity, the said Bobbie W. Jett does hereby release the said Hank Williams from any and all further claims arising out of her condition or the birth of said child."

After their marriage, Daddy and Billie Jean rented a house in Bossier City, on the same street — Modica Street — where we had lived in 1948 and 1949. Billy Jean tried to assume the responsibility of taking care of Daddy, but the situation was out of her hands.

She could not be the person he longed for her to be, and he was unable to be much of a husband. Their lives together were pretty much of a nightmare.

Mrs. Stone was distrustful of Billie Jean's lack of experience in dealing with Daddy's problems and, therefore, did not bow out of her son's life as she had done when Mother had come onto the scene. Bob McKinnon remembers receiving a phone call from Lillie Stone in fall 1952, asking for his help in an awkward situation. Daddy was drunk in a motel in Cape Girardeau, Missouri. His mother had hired an ambulance plane to go and pick him up, but she was concerned about protecting him until she could get there. Bob phoned the sheriff in that town and explained that Daddy was a very sick man and asked if there was any way someone could look in on him.

The sheriff immediately took a doctor over to the motel and put a deputy outside the room until Mrs. Stone could get there with the plane.

And still Daddy worked. He was kept going by Toby Marshall's treatments and running on the last of his strength. When Daddy became very ill and missed a show on the second night of a Texas tour in December, they sent for his mother. She stayed on for the remainder of the schedule, which ended up on December 21 at the Skyline Club in Austin.

"Grand Ole Opry" star Billy Walker was just an up-and-coming singer on the "Louisiana Hayride" at the time, and he jumped at the chance to be part of that Texas tour.

> I talked to Hank a lot on that trip. He told me he'd already made the deal to go back to the Opry in February. He said he was going to get rid of Billie Jean and try to get Audrey back and get his life straightened out. He told me that he knew he was in bad shape and he wanted to get away from this doctor whose hold on him was drugs. He said he was going down to the Bahamas and check himself in somewhere down there. He knew his body was messed up, and he wanted desperately to try to get it straightened out. I think he had been physically attracted to Billie Jean, but he wanted to go home. He told me he could never love no one but Audrey.
>
> I think Hank Williams had a self-destructive attitude about his life from his childhood, because he talked an awful lot about his childhood and it wasn't a very pretty picture. I believe this carried over into his manhood, and he never cared whether he lived or died. When people are put in a position where they don't think much of their own life, it seems like they race to destroy it.
>
> All the time that we were together, I didn't see him eat but half a hamburger on two or three occasions. Now, we're talking about ten or twelve days. He got worse and worse as time went on. I didn't know this guy Toby Marshall was a quack doctor at the time. I asked him what he was giving Hank, and he said he was giving him pure adrenalin. I didn't know what adrenalin was, and he had some of these little pink three-sided pills that he was giving him, too, and I come to find out they were pep pills.

✻　✻　✻　✻　✻

> Somebody now would gladly give his life
> To bring back the sweet used to be.

And try to repay all the wrong he has done,
Somebody's lonesome, and that somebody's me.

❀   ❀   ❀   ❀   ❀

I was just eleven when Daddy took me and Hank, Jr., over to the Parthenon in Nashville in his new blue convertible. Another man was with him, but I don't remember who it was.

On the way back home, I said, "Daddy, Mother lets me drive now. She sits next to me, but I do the driving. Would you let me drive your car the rest of the way home?"

"Your mother lets you drive?" he asked.

I said, "Yes, sir. I can work the pedals, but you would have to sit here next to me."

"If she lets you do it, you can," he said. So I crawled over there and he sat next to me and I drove the car the rest of the way home.

That was the last time I can remember seeing him.

CHAPTER 11

Just Say God's Called Home Your Ramblin' Man

Just before Daddy died, he called and asked if he could come home. Mother said yes. He had put Billie Jean on an airplane and told her he was going back to his family, where he belonged. I remember Mother coming into the back room and telling Miss Ragland that Daddy was coming home, and she wanted them to get the house ready.

Daddy's cousin Marie Harvell remembers that sometime during the week before Christmas Daddy had gone to buy Hank, Jr., a train for Christmas, and Billie Jean threw a fit about it. However, it is uncertain exactly when Daddy sent her home. About that time, Daddy had confided to his friend, M. C. Jarrett, "I ain't got nothin' but just my guitar and a wife, and I wish to hell I didn't have nothin' but a guitar."

It is clear that Daddy was back at his mother's boardinghouse in Montgomery before Christmas because Brack Schuffert was visiting him there every day. Schuffert says that the phone at the boardinghouse was ringing every five minutes with "somebody wanting him to buy them a radio station or sing one of their songs." Daddy told him, "Brack, I can't rest. That phone rings continuously wherever I go. I wish I was off somewhere by myself." Schuffert told him he didn't have to keep up that terrible pace. He could just write songs, record, and stay off the road, but Daddy said that wasn't possible. He was already booked up through May.

109

On December 28 Daddy played his last show, performing at the Elite Cafe in Montgomery for a musicians' union dinner. *The Alabama Journal* reported that "another special star of the show the musicians put on for themselves was a thin, tired-looking, ex-country boy with a guitar . . . Hank Williams."

A few months earlier, Daddy had told a reporter for the *Tennessean* in Nashville, "I will never live long enough for you to write a story about me."

              o   o   o   o   o

> I'm not gonna worry wrinkles in my brow,
> 'Cause nothin's ever gonna be alright nohow,
> No matter how I struggle and strive,
> I'll never get out of this world alive.

              o   o   o   o   o

Charles Carr was a seventeen-year-old freshman at Auburn University home for the holidays when Daddy asked his father, Daniel, to let Charles act as Daddy's chauffeur for two shows scheduled on December 31 in Charleston, West Virginia, and January 1 in Canton, Ohio. Charles's father only consented after he had determined that Daddy was not drinking too heavily.

The two left on the afternoon of Tuesday, December 30, headed for Charleston and Canton via Birmingham, Alabama, and Chattanooga and Knoxville, Tennessee. The weather was already turning bad and progress was slow, so they stayed the night in Birmingham. The next morning they drove on to Knoxville.

The rest of the story of Wednesday, December 31, 1952, the last day of Daddy's life, was documented in a handwritten police report filed by Tennessee Highway Patrolman Swann H. Kitts, who stopped Charles Carr for reckless driving just before midnight.

According to Kitts's investigation, Daddy and Carr left the blue Cadillac at the airport at 3:30 P.M. and caught a plane out of Knoxville for Charleston, West Virginia. Bad weather prevented the plane from landing, and it returned to Knoxville. They arrived back at 5:57 P.M. and drove over to the Andrew Johnson Hotel, where Carr checked them in at 7:08 P.M. Kitts stated in his report that Daddy was drunk and spoke only a few words when porters carried him up to his room. Carr ordered two steaks, one for himself and one for Daddy, but Daddy was passed out and could not eat.

Then, continued Kitts, "Dr. P. H. Cardwell arrived. He said Williams was very drunk and that he talked with him. He gave Williams two injections of morphine and Vitamin B-12." The doctor noticed that Daddy had three or four capsules, but didn't know what they were or how many he might have taken. Cardwell stayed a short time and left.

Somewhere during the next one and one half to two hours, Kitts wrote, Carr talked with someone who instructed him to leave Knoxville immediately and drive on to Canton, Ohio. It was too late for them to make the New Year's show in Charleston, so they were to head directly to Canton. Carr and the porters dressed Daddy, and "he was lifeless as they put his clothes on him. The porters carried him out and put him on the back seat of the car. Williams never moved at all. He seemed to make a coughing-like sound (only twice) as they carried him, but was lifeless and didn't move."

Carr checked them out of the hotel at 10:45 P.M. and about 11:45 he was stopped just outside of Knoxville by Kitts after the blue Cadillac almost hit the patrol car head on. (Carr explained later that he was attempting to pass a truck, decided against it at the last minute because of the road conditions, and had trouble getting back into the lane because another car had come up close on the truck after he pulled out to pass.) Kitts walked up to the car, shined his light in the back seat, and "I noticed Williams and asked Carr if he could be dead, as he was pale and blue-looking. But he said Williams had drank six bottles of beer, and a doctor had given him two injections to help him sleep." Carr asked Kitts not to wake him, as he was very sick.

Kitts took Carr to Rutledge, where he wrote him a ticket at 12:30 A.M. for reckless driving. Carr was tried before Justice of the Peace O. H. Marshall and fined twenty-five dollars plus court costs. Kitts talked to Carr in the presence of Marshall and Sheriff J. N. Antrican about Daddy's condition, and they all noticed Carr seemed a little nervous. Again, Carr requested that Daddy not be disturbed. Kitts also notes that a soldier was in the car when it was stopped. Carr left Rutledge about 1:00 A.M.

"After investigating this matter," Kitts concluded, "I think that Williams was dead when he was dressed and carried out of the hotel. Since he was drunk and was given the injections and could have taken some capsules earlier, he couldn't have lasted over an hour and a half or two hours.

"A man drunk or doped will make some movement if you move them. A dead man will make a coughing sound if they are lifted around. Taking all this into consideration, he must have died in Knoxville in the hotel."

That New Year's Eve in Nashville, Fred Rose and his son, Wesley, were offering a toast to Daddy — he was coming back, Mother was attending a New Year's party with promoter A. V. Bamford's wife, Maxine (Bamford was the agent handling the Charleston and Canton shows for Daddy), Miss Ragland was assembling the train that Daddy had sent to Hank, Jr., for Christmas, and I was spending the night with my friends Freda and Mark Garrett.

According to Carr, it was several hours before he became suspicious enough to check on Daddy himself. When he stopped the car and tried to rouse him, Daddy was cold to the touch. Carr raced to the nearest hospital, in Beckley, West Virginia, where a doctor informed him that Daddy was already dead. Since there was no coroner on staff there, Carr would have to drive on to the hospital in Oak Hill.

At 7:00 A.M. on January 1, 1953, Daddy was declared dead at the Oak Hill Hospital in Oak Hill, West Virginia, by Dr. Diego Nunnari, and his body was taken to Tyree's Funeral Home on Main Street. Charles Carr called his father in Montgomery, and Daniel Carr notified Mrs. Stone.

Dr. Malinin, a pathologist at Beckley Hospital, performed the autopsy, which showed that Daddy had suffered hemorrhages in his heart and neck. Alcohol was found in the bloodstream, but, mysteriously, no evidence of narcotics was found. The death certificate, filed in Fayetteville, West Virginia, the county seat, listed the place of death as Oak Hill and the cause of death as "acute right ventricular dilation." Lillie Stone and Toby Marshall, who had been waiting in Charleston, arrived in

Above: Daddy on High Life, his Tennessee Walking Horse. *Below:*
Mother and Daddy gave Trigger to me on my ninth birthday.

Above: Daddy and Mother with the most famous version of the Drifting Cowboys band. Left to right are Howard Watts (Cedric Rainwater) on bass, Jerry Rivers on fiddle, Mother, Daddy, Sammy Pruett, and Don Helms on steel. *Left:* Daddy leaving the Opry backstage, August 1952.

Two of the last photos ever taken of Daddy while he was alive.

Above left: After Daddy died, Mother visited Lake Kowaliga, where Daddy had written one of his last songs, "Kaw-Liga." *Above right:* Daddy's mother, Lillie Stone, visited the lake with Mother. *Left:* Mother dedicated the wooden Indian that still stands at Lake Kowaliga in memory of the song "Kaw-Liga." [Photos courtesy of Bob McKinnon]

Above: We posed in the den for this family photograph in front of the display of Daddy's hit records. *Right:* Our nanny, Miss Audrey Ragland.

Lycrecia Ann and Randall Hank Will

Left: Daddy would have loved this picture taken soon after he died. *Below:* Hank, Jr., and Mother, wearing one of her trademark "A" outfits, pose following one of his early stage appearances.

Mother was really excited when she caught this magnificent sailfish while we were vacationing in Florida. She later had it mounted on the wall in the den of the house on Franklin Road.

Left: A promotional photograph taken for my brief show business career. *Below:* Sitting in my first car, a 1956 Chevrolet Bel-aire convertible, on our Franklin Road property.

Above: From left to right are Oscar Davis, Jim Denny, Doris Davis, Dollie Denny, and Mother. *Below:* Mother with Eddie Crandall.

Above: Mother and Hank, Jr., at my 1960 wedding to Lamar Morris. *Below:* Mother and her baby sister Lynette.

Right: An early publicity photo of Hank, Jr., approximately age fourteen. *Below:* A photograph taken during the second Hank Williams Day in Montgomery, Alabama, in 1957. Included in the picture are the Everly Brothers, Cornelia Folsom (later Mrs. George Wallace) between them, me, T. Tommy Cutrer (standing), Mother, Ruby Folsom, and Irene and J. T. Smith (Daddy's sister and her husband).

Left: Hank, Jr., and Mother toward the end of their professional relationship. *Below:* Me at a party with my friend Carla Norrell.

Above: Mother with George Hamilton and Susan Oliver during the filming of *Your Cheatin' Heart. Below:* Mother and one of her versions of her all-girl band, The Cold, Cold Hearts.

Above left: Flossie Morris, our cook, who helped run our household and raise Hank, Jr., and me. *Above right:* Loretta and Harold Fleming stayed in Montana while Hank, Jr., was recovering from his terrible fall. *Below:* At my daughter Tawana's wedding, left to right, are my children Ricky, Tawana, me, and Michelle.

Above: At my daughter Tawana's wedding to Jim Askins; left to right are Lamar Morris (her father), Tawana, Jim, and me. *Below left:* My husband Norris Hoover and me at our home in Charlotte, North Carolina. *Below right:* With one of my best friends, Delila Ellis.

Left: Mother and Daddy the way I'd like to remember them. *Below:* Mother and Daddy's graves in Montgomery, Alabama.

Oak Hill the next morning, January 2, and Billie Jean, her father, and her brother arrived soon after. Daddy was dressed in a white cowboy suit for his last ride back to Montgomery.

Mother was expecting Daddy home soon. Miss Ragland remembers when Mother got the call. "Somebody upstairs answered the phone when they called to say he had died. Mrs. Williams came in the room and told me that he was dead. I could not believe it, but she said, 'Yes, Hank is dead.' Then she went all to pieces."

    ✿   ✿   ✿   ✿   ✿

> Darling, let's turn back the years,
> And go back to yesterday,
> Let's pretend that time has stopped,
> And I didn't go away.

    ✿   ✿   ✿   ✿   ✿

In Canton, Ohio, Don Helms stood silently backstage as the emcee "announced to the stunned crowd that Hank Williams, 'King of the Hillbillies,' had died en route to the city." The *Canton Repository* reported that "while a single spotlight played on the drawn curtains, fans . . . joined with the entire cast to sing 'I Saw the Light!' Then the show went on. . . . That was the way he would have wanted it."

    ✿   ✿   ✿   ✿   ✿

> I saw the light, I saw the light,
> No more darkness, no more night,
> Now I'm so happy, no sorrow in sight,
> Praise the Lord, I saw the light.

    ✿   ✿   ✿   ✿   ✿

Bernice Turner, remembers when she first heard of Daddy's death. "I was down on the floor cutting out a dress when the news came over the radio. I just started screaming and crying. I just could not believe that had happened. When we were all together, we were together night and day. We became like a family, and I loved these people. When we were with him, I'd get angry because I couldn't understand — like Audrey couldn't understand — why he couldn't just stay sober. I thought he was just mean. But I could not believe that he had died."

Daddy's mortal remains were brought back to Montgomery, and he lay at first in his mother's boardinghouse, where his family and closest friends gathered in their sorrow. Together in the same house, united by the emotional upheaval of the moment, were Lillie Stone, Billie Jean, Bobbie Jett, and Mother.

A. V. Bamford handled the funeral arrangements. He notified the police and fire departments of the family's desire to use the Montgomery Municipal Auditorium for the memorial services. Then he put in the calls to Nashville, to Daddy's friends at the "Grand Ole Opry," and together they planned the musical tributes for the funeral program.

"The night before the funeral," remembers Brack Schuffert, "Hank was laying in the front room up there at his mother's boardinghouse. I was letting people in and out the door; there was a huge crowd outside. Mr. Williams — Hank's daddy — needed someone to take him to the florist to get some flowers for his son. I carried him up to Rosemont Gardens, but they were closed. It was about 11:00 at night, but they were still working getting all the flowers ready for the funeral. We knocked on the side door for about ten minutes, and somebody finally came back there and said, 'We're closed.'

"I said, 'I understand that, but I've got Hank Williams' daddy out here, and he wants you to make him a spray of flowers to put on Hank's grave.'

"They said, 'Well, yes sir, we'll let you in. What size flowers do you want?'

"'I'm a poor man,' the old man told them. 'All I can afford is five dollars.'"

Sunday, January 4, 1953, was a cold day in Montgomery, Alabama. There had not been such a large gathering of people there since Jefferson Davis had been sworn in as President of the Confederacy in 1861. Only 2,750 were able to jam inside the Municipal Auditorium, and an estimated 25,000 people stood outside as the service began at 2:30 P.M. *The Nashville Banner* reported that "the thousands who streamed past his open casket . . . were proof that the followers of Hank Williams knew no class barriers."

Dr. Henry L. Lyon, pastor of the Highland Avenue Baptist Church in Montgomery, officiated, and he was assisted by an old family friend, Reverend Talmadge Smith of the Ramer Baptist Church. Ernest Tubb opened the service with the emotional spiritual, one of Daddy's favorites, "Beyond The Sunset." The congregation was led in prayer, and then Dr. Lyon delivered his eulogy:

> Hank Williams, the singing idol of millions of Americans, has just answered the call of the "last round-up." Even so, if this world should last a thousand years, Hank shall remain dear to millions of hearts. I cannot preach the funeral of Hank Williams. It has already been preached in music and song on the radio — listened to by millions of admiring Americans since the sad message of his death was announced Thursday. The preacher of the message — Hank Williams, the congregation — the American people. His life is a real personification of what can happen in this country to one little insignificant speck of humanity. Upon hearing of Hank's death the other day, one of our good people of Montgomery has been quoted as saying, amid his tears, "Why, Hank used to shine my shoes." Yes, Hank shined this man's shoes and thousands of other's shoes. Even then he was singing with every snap and pop of his brush and rag. We shall ever remember the man who climbed from the shoeshine stand to the heights of immortal glory in the hearts of all people who loved Hank and his special brand of folk music. We thank God for our great American country which gives us the privilege to sing like we want to sing and the privilege to listen to our own special kind of music — enjoying it with the entirety of our being.
>
> Millions and millions will never tire of the genuine heart appeal of his songs. As long as we have America with all its freedom to succeed, we will have our Hank Williams to inspire us in the midst of life's hardships.
>
> Hank Williams was a great American. What was the secret of his greatness? Listen, I'll tell you what it was — he had a message. It was swelling in him like a great body of water behind a massive dam. It was a message of the heart. Deep down in the citadel of his inner being there was desire, burden, fear, ambition, reverse after reverse, bitter disappointment, joy, success, sympathy, love for people. It was all there in Hank's heart. The break had to come, it did come. It came with Hank Williams playing on his guitar, singing only as a free-born American can sing. When he

played on his guitar, he played on the heart strings of millions of Americans. They listened to Hank over the radio in their homes, in the bus station, in the car driving along the highway, in the prison, in the office. They listened everywhere — white and colored, rich and poor, the illiterate and the educated, the young and the old. Yes, we all listened and we'll still listen. Why?

Hank had a message. This message was written in the language of all the people. It was a message of the things that everyone feels — life itself. Years ago, one of American's greatest doctors said, "If you have something which represents a genuine need of humanity, though you live in a cottage, deep in the forest, mankind will beat a trail to your door." Hank Williams did have something that humanity universally needs — a song with a heart-felt message.

I guess I was the only one who wasn't there. Mother's sister Lynette was a teen-ager at the time, and her clearest memory is of Roy Acuff. Roy began by saying, "We'd like to do this song as Hank wanted it done," and proceeded to lead a choir of "Grand Ole Opry" stars, including Red Foley, Little Jimmy Dickens, Carl Smith, Eddie Hill, Lew Childre, Webb Pierce, Johnnie Wright, and Jack Anglin, in the singing of "I Saw The Light." Red Foley sang "Peace In The Valley" as he had promised Daddy he would if Daddy died first, and "tears streamed down Foley's face as he struggled to finish the song without breaking up." Just before the benediction, the Statesmen Quartet sang "Precious Memories," and the service ended.

      ❂   ❂   ❂   ❂   ❂

In the world of sorrow I've seen trouble and woe,
When I get to glory I'll see no more.
For I know my prayers have not been in vain,
When I get to glory I'm gonna sing, sing, sing.

      ❂   ❂   ❂   ❂   ❂

The pallbearers, Jim Denny, A. V. Bamford, Jack Anglin, Johnnie Wright, Bill Smith, W. Louis King, Bob Helton, and Braxton Schuffert, lifted the heavy casket into the hearse. Attending were the honorary pallbearers, including the entire staffs of WSM, WSFA, and KWKH radio, Fred and Wesley Rose, and Jerry Rivers. Thousands lined the route the funeral

procession traveled on its way to the Oakwood Cemetery An-
nex, where Daddy was laid to rest. One hundred policemen
and firemen were on hand to keep order and to help the
mourners make their way through the crowd. From the cemetery, the family members returned to the boardinghouse.

✿   ✿   ✿   ✿   ✿

Let me travel this land from the mountains to the sea.
'Cause that's the life I believe He meant for me.
And when I'm gone and at my grave you stand,
Just say God's called home your ramblin' man.

CHAPTER 12

I'll Carry on in the Same Old Way

It took a long time for it to register with me that Daddy was really dead. Mother understood it right away, but she never did get over it. She blamed herself that Daddy passed away so young because of her part in the divorce. My Mother did not let people know how she really felt inside, though. She portrayed a strong image to people when she was out in public, but Mother was very, very sad.

Since meeting Daddy in 1943, Mother's energies had always been focused on him, whether she was promoting his career, organizing his affairs, or keeping him out of trouble. She had had a short burst of freedom throughout the year they were separated, including a plan to form an all-girl band and make a name for herself as a single in show business, but Daddy's death ended all of that.

Mother's self-respect had been seriously damaged. In addition to the years she had spent as a wife who couldn't get Daddy to quit drinking, her public reputation had gone downhill. Sympathy for Daddy grew even stronger as his fans and friends watched his tragic downfall, and Mother's own outbursts of temper and attentions to other men did not improve what they thought of her. Finally, Daddy's last act of spite, his marriage to Billie Jean on the stage of the civic auditorium in New Orleans, was very humiliating to her. Daddy's funeral, with Billie Jean, not her, as his widow, had to be even more crushing.

Another matter severely undermined Mother's ability to recover her sense of balance. Along with the legacies of music
and passion that Daddy left for her, she had also inherited the
effects of his alcoholism. I have learned that the closer someone
is to an alcoholic, the more that person develops a certain way
of thinking and reacting and acquires emotional scars that will
last throughout life. The experts call this condition "co-dependency," and even though it comes from the stress of living with
an alcoholic, it eventually becomes a disease of its own. Unfortunately, many co-dependents who are unable to cope with
their problems turn toward drinking or drug use themselves.

Two days after Daddy's funeral, on January 6, 1953, a baby
girl named Antha Belle Jett was born to Bobbie Jett in
Montgomery. Within the month, Bobbie had gone to Califor-
nia, leaving her baby with Mrs. Stone as the arrangements
Daddy had signed two and a half months earlier called for.
That was more humiliation for Mother.

In an effort to escape the pain and guilt that she was feeling,
Mother once more became Mrs. Hank Williams. She welcomed the attention and the opportunity to express her love for
Daddy. She went right back to doing what she had in the years
before the divorce, rather than trying to recover from the
awful shock of the tragedy. "Since he has gone," she wrote, "his
memory is still like the dreams he made come true for me. I will
try to carry on where he left off. The world of music was his; I
am making it mine. I will try to find happiness in the world in
which he found it and gave it to me."

The sweeping forces that would make it very hard for
Mother to ever find happiness again were already in motion.
As the inspiration behind Daddy's songs, the recipient of half
his royalties, and the mother of his children, she was placed at
the center of the whirlwind.

The public's appetite for anything associated with Daddy
reached a fever pitch within weeks after his death. At the time
of Daddy's death, his single "I'll Never Get Out Of This World
Alive," was climbing the charts. The song tore his fans apart.
But that wasn't all. The *Billboard* reported in late January that
the MGM pressing plant in Bloomfield, New Jersey, was having trouble keeping up with the demand for all of Daddy's re-

cordings — fifty singles and two albums — and was operating around the clock to meet the orders that kept pouring in.

Deejays were flooding the airwaves with Daddy's music, programming it for one or two hours at a time. Acuff-Rose was working twenty-four hours a day, too, printing copies of Daddy's two songbooks, and MGM was also swamped with hundreds of requests every week for photographs.

Everybody knew Daddy's relationship with Mother had influenced his songwriting, and his fans were fascinated with the idea that she was his inspiration. However, the songs with titles such as "Cold, Cold Heart," "Your Cheatin' Heart," and "I'm So Lonesome I Could Cry" gave some people the idea that Mother was the one to blame for all of his problems.

Mother got asked a lot about whether she was Daddy's inspiration. By 1973 she had learned to be cautious with her answers: "Hank wrote the songs himself — whether or not I was an inspiration, I will leave that up to other people. I know within me and I know what Hank told me on a number of occasions, but I'd rather leave that up to the public to judge because I've been criticized on some songs — it's so unjust, it's unreal."

       ❖   ❖   ❖   ❖   ❖

Are you writing any songs for me up in Heaven,
The way you always did down here.
Have you told the angels how much I love you,
And tho you're gone you still seem so near.

Are you writing any songs for me up in Heaven,
So when I meet you beyond the blue,
You'll say 'Come here and listen to me,'
Then I'll smile and listen just as we used to do . . .
— Audrey Williams

       ❖   ❖   ❖   ❖   ❖

The royalties were pouring in from MGM and Acuff-Rose greater than they ever had before, but this only complicated the legal situations Mother had to face. Daddy left no will, so beginning only days after his death, the legal battles were on. Those battles have not been stilled even thirty-six years later.

Mrs. Stone filed the first court action in early January, asking to be named administratrix of Daddy's estate. She had all of his belongings, including the titles to his two Cadillacs, which he had signed over to her. All the possible heirs were named: Audrey, Randall (Hank, Jr.), Billie Jean, Lon Williams, Lillie Stone, Irene, and me. My name was removed from the list when it was learned I had never been adopted by Daddy. Mrs. Stone raised the question of the legality of Daddy's marriage to Billie Jean. "She is trying to cheat me out of everything, but I think she will fail," complained Billie Jean.

Later that month, Lillie Stone was named administratrix of Daddy's Alabama estate, which she estimated at only five thousand dollars, including a four thousand dollar cashier's check, but not the cars which Daddy had already deeded to her. In addition, a Shreveport judge ruled that Billie Jean's marriage to Daddy was illegal because her divorce from her first husband was not final until October 29, eleven days after their first wedding ceremony and ten days after the other two.

After some more minor bickering with Mrs. Stone about a copy of Daddy's autopsy report and the cars, Billie Jean started in on Mother. In January she had disputed Mother's claims that Daddy was planning a reconciliation with his family. She said she had returned to Bossier City only to sell their furniture and pack their belongings before joining him in Nashville. Considering herself the rightful widow, she filed a suit in April in the district court in Minden, Louisiana, seeking to prevent Mother from using the name "Mrs. Hank Williams" or to be paid one hundred thousand dollars for damages "suffered because the defendant has usurped her exclusive right to use the name of Mrs. Hank Williams." In spite of that, Mother appeared with a "Grand Ole Opry" troupe in New Orleans, where she said only that "she had been using the name for ten years."

In May it was Mother's turn to seek the assistance of the courts. She petitioned the court in Nashville to allow Acuff-Rose and MGM to continue paying her the fifty percent of Daddy's royalties she had been receiving since the divorce. The agreement she and Daddy had made did not specify what would happen in the event of Daddy's death and/or remarriage. The remaining fifty percent of the estate was also tied up because he had died without a will.

Billie Jean was next. In June she filed a suit in a Nashville federal court to have "certain royalties, monies and proceeds from contracts" amounting to $33,218.34 paid to her. She also sought an injunction to prevent Mother from collecting from Acuff-Rose or MGM, asking that a receiver be appointed to take charge of the funds until the court could give a decision.

Round one ended in August 1953, when Equity Judge William J. Wade of the Davidson County Chancery Court in Nashville recognized the property settlement between Mother and Daddy as binding even after his death. Randall Hank Williams was declared the principal heir, and his fifty percent of the estate was to be distributed by Mrs. Stone as part of her role as administratrix. The estate settled with Billie Jean by paying her thirty to forty thousand dollars for "all of her claims and rights."

In the midst of mourning and the anxiety of the unresolved legal issues, Mother still, of course, had to take care of Hank, Jr., and me. About one month after Daddy died, she hired Flossie Morris to live at the house, cook for us, and help Miss Ragland in running the household whenever Mother had to be gone. Flossie remembers when she first knew Mother right after she had come back from Montgomery and burying Daddy.

> She talked about him a lot. I got to feeling like I knew him — all the pictures, all the things she'd say about him. She said she loved him, and he was supposed to come back home. It took her a long time not to be sad anymore. I don't think she ever got over it. She wished they hadn't gotten a divorce, and I asked her, "It wasn't your fault, was it?" and she told me, "Yes, it was." She would say how much she loved him, and she wished they hadn't separated. She'd say he was a good, kind man.

With Flossie and Miss Ragland around to take care of Hank, Jr., and me, Mother felt freer to travel. She had to be present at many of the legal proceedings, and she was requested to appear at nearly all the tribute shows for Daddy. Like other mothers on the road, though, she worried about us when she wasn't there to supervise. She called home frequently and spoiled us with generous gifts when she returned. "She was just crazy about her kids," says Flossie.

The first of many tribute shows dedicated to Daddy's memory was "Kaw-Liga Day," held on March 18, 1953, at Lake Martin where Daddy had written one of his last and greatest songs, "Kaw-Liga." Bob McKinnon, the Alexander City disc jockey who had stayed with Daddy at the lake, and Bob's friend, Jim Watley, had come up with a plan to help popularize the new Kowaliga State Park on Lake Martin by staging a Hank Williams memorial show. They called Mother, and she was delighted with the idea.

There were three shows that day, and a capacity crowd of twelve hundred was at each one. The troupe of performers from the "Grand Ole Opry" included George Morgan, Autry Inman, Stringbean, Radio Dot and Smokey, and, of course, Audrey Williams. Mother was featured in the dedication ceremony when a wooden statue of an Indian was placed in the park in memory of Daddy and his song. The mayor of Alexander City also presented a framed, tinted photograph of the lake, commemorating the song and the occasion, to Mrs. Stone.

Mother looked gorgeous in a black suede cowgirl costume with a rhinestone "A" on the front of the skirt. She told reporters she had decided not to put a band together, but to work as a single, and would be appearing with Red Foley and his band in New Orleans in April, and later with Carl Smith for two weeks in Canada. When they asked if she enjoyed that kind of work, she replied quietly, "Yes, I like it, I guess. It's something to do . . . to keep me busy."

The Alexander City Outlook reported that "she appeared nervous while talking to the audience before singing each number, but regained her composure and went through the numbers in fine style, exhibiting some of the undulating tones made famous by her ex-husband."

After the show, one elderly lady commented, "Hank Williams may be gone, but he's more popular than ever." That was both sad and funny because just a few months earlier, he had boasted to a fellow musician, "Look friend, I could draw a better crowd dead than you can alive."

An advertisement in the May 2 *Billboard* described "The One And Only Audrey (Mrs. Hank) Williams" as "the girl for whom the late, great Hank Williams wrote his famous songs" and stated that she was available, through promoter A. V.

Bamford, as a single or with an all-star show for appearances at auditoriums, parks, fairs, theaters, or on TV. And appear she did.

The appearance at Alexander City for "Kaw-Liga Day" was the third stop of a tour Mother was making with the same Opry group. They had been in Montgomery and Calhoun City, Mississippi, on the previous day. Next, they went on to New Orleans in April, then to parks and drive-ins in Ohio and Pennsylvania during June, followed by dates in Canada, Texas, and Oklahoma.

In August, on a tour through Maryland, her show broke the attendance record at the New River Ranch at Rising Sun. Also in August, she was signed, along with the Texas Cowgirls Basketball Team, for six months work with Worldwide Sports Attractions to begin in October. They were scheduled to travel through the U.S., Canada, Alaska, and Europe. In December she played a number of dates on the West Coast, talked to several studios interested in producing a film on Daddy, and was a guest in the home of Mr. and Mrs. Roy Rogers.

Mother revealed a lot of what she was feeling at this time in her third Decca recording session, in August 1953. Still backed by the Drifting Cowboys, but short one guitar player, she recorded three emotional numbers that day. First was a recitation of Daddy's, "To My Pal Bocephus," a poem filled with a father's hopes and concerns for his baby son. She read the words just as Daddy would have done, without changing the wording for the speaker as a "man" and a "father." Her second number, "I Forgot More Than You'll Ever Know About Him," a current hit at the time for the Davis Sisters, was so appropriate to her feelings about Billie Jean's claims to Daddy that it might have been written just for her. For the last song, Mother rewrote the lyrics to Daddy's "Rambling' Man" to express some of her own thoughts:

     ✿   ✿   ✿   ✿   ✿

> Some folks might say that I didn't care,
> But wherever you went I was always there.
> When I get lonely, at your grave I'll stand.
> So I'll be near my ramblin' man.
> I still love you honey and I can't understand
> I'm a ramblin' gal that lost her ramblin' man.

     ✿   ✿   ✿   ✿   ✿

Daddy had been known to be very generous, and some people remember that Mother's generosity increased at this time, especially toward anyone who had befriended Daddy. Bob McKinnon recalls that "after Hank died, Audrey tried her best to do what she could for Hank's friends. At the time she knew that I was getting a little ambitious about working on a bigger radio station. So she called me one day in 1953 and wanted to know if I could come to Nashville. She thought she had a job for me through the program director at station WLAC. I went up there and she called the man while we were at a restaurant and made arrangements for him to meet with me the following Monday morning. I never went, though, I admit I blew the whole thing."

☼　☼　☼　☼　☼

You know honey it's been a year now
Since we got together for a little talk.
I was sitting here thinking of how
We first met for that first walk,
That's how I started my life with you.

Yes Hank, I remember when we first met,
You were working on a medicine show
In my hometown, I'll never forget
I happened to drive by and we said hello,
That's how I started my life with you.

I acted foolish and played hard to get,
I had never heard of you then, little did I know
You were singing me love songs and playing a part,
Soon on the strings of your guitar, you won my heart.

Twas in Andalusia, Alabama, December 15 year of 44
I became your bride, remember how I cried.
Couldn't find a preacher so we married in a store,
Without a honeymoon to run away and hide,
That's how I started my life with you.

The next few years a little rough, not too long,
We worked hard and waited for that day,
Then you began to sing a certain song,
The Lovesick Blues paved the way,
That's how I started my life with you.

About the time that fame had begun,
The Grand Ole Opry in Nashville called you,

That was the year of 49, God gave us a son,
Life was complete, a girl like me a boy like you.
That's how I started my life with you.

But our happiness didn't last too long,
People began to wagging their tongues
And you and I just couldn't seem to get along,
So you began to writing more and more songs,
That's how I started my life with you.

Along about then, everything went wrong,
Little did we know it wouldn't be long
'Til you'd be in Heaven no more to be blue,
It's hard to go on without my life with you.

Well Honey, it's time for me to go.
I can see a bright star shining.
It's you to guide me, I know,
To that gold and silver lining,
Then I can go on with my life with you.

❖   ❖   ❖   ❖   ❖

In the early part of 1954, the pattern of Mother's life without
Daddy began to be clear. She had easily adapted herself to the
high life and fast pace that allowed her to forget her loneliness
in the midst of friends and parties.

Doris Noles was Mother's secretary and friend during the
early fifties. Doris worked out at our house on Franklin Road.
She paid the bills, kept up the correspondence, and traveled
with Mother to collect the money out on the road. "Audrey
wasn't a happy person," Doris recalls. "Even all the money she
had didn't make her happy."

By mid-February Mother and a "Grand Ole Opry" troupe
including Hank Snow, Slim Whitman, and Webb Pierce had
completed a tour of California, Arizona, New Mexico, Texas,
and Colorado. They stopped to spend a few days resting at the
posh Broadmoor Hotel in Colorado Springs.

Doris was there, along with promoter Oscar Davis, who had
put together the tour. Doris and Oscar, who were soon to be
married, were part of the gathering that assembled for an early
celebration of Mother's thirty-first birthday. Doris remembers
that night at the Broadmoor in Colorado Springs.

It had a great big terrace with all kinds of greenery, flowers, glass-topped tables, and skylights. Audrey and I decided to go down and have a drink to celebrate her birthday. Everybody kept joining us until there were about fifteen or twenty people there. They were ordering champagne, and Oscar was clowning. He was pretending it was a wake, and he got up on a glass-topped table and went through it. There was glass all over the place. When someone tried to order another bottle of champagne, we were told that the manager said to cut us off. At that point, Oscar said, "Well, when you're in Europe and you drink champagne, you throw the glass in the fireplace." They didn't have a fireplace, so they started throwing glasses up against the wall. Then we were asked to leave.

At the same time, Jim Denny, head of the Artists' Bureau at the Opry, happened to call the hotel to book rooms for some executives from National Life. They said, "We don't want any more of those Opry people. We just had to throw a bunch of them out of this hotel." Of course, that embarrassed him and he called everyone back to Nashville. Oh, he was mad!

"Audrey loved to party," recalls Doris. "We'd just be sitting there, and she'd say, 'Let's have a party.' She'd get on the phone and start calling people, and I'd get the booze and chips. We had a lot of fun."

There was another unfortunate incident in Colorado Springs. During a snowstorm, the car Mother was driving skidded on some ice and crashed into two stalled cars and a gasoline truck. No one was hurt in the accident, but the car was badly wrecked.

Then, in mid-March, a fire broke out in our house and caused thousands of dollars in damages. It was cold, and a storm had knocked out the electricity, so Mother and Miss Ragland decided to build a fire. We didn't have any wood, so they put a large cardboard box, the size of the fireplace opening, in to burn, and it flamed up and burnt the whole front of the mantle. Moments later, the house was filled with smoke and flames. The master bath was hit hard, half of the attic was gutted, and a large section of the roof was burned through. A lot of Mother's wardrobe, including her stage costumes, was destroyed by fire, smoke, and water. She was just about to

leave on a tour of Michigan and Ohio, where her streak of bad
luck would continue.

In Muskegon, Michigan, seventy-five hundred dollars in
cash was stolen from a cigar box left in Mother's car. The
money was the advance sales receipts for the show underway
that night in the high school auditorium. A twenty-two caliber
pistol was also taken from the car. "Mrs. Williams insisted she
locked all the doors," stated the newspaper report "but the
front door next to the driver's seat was found unlocked when
Miss Doris Noles, her secretary, went to the car to get money
wrappers about 10:00 P.M." Fingerprints were taken of all
members of the touring group, but none matched the ones on
the cigar box, and the money was never recovered.

The biggest of all the tributes to Daddy was the first "Hank
Williams Day," held on September 20–21, 1954, in Montgomery, Alabama. It drew over one hundred of country music's
greatest artists, three state governors, and crowds of nearly
fifty thousand people to honor Daddy's memory.

The two-day event was sponsored and planned by the Alcazar Shrine Temple. The program opened on the evening of
the twentieth, with three dances at the Ft. Dixie Bibb Graves
Hall, the Alcazar Temple, and the City Auditorium.

At eleven the next morning Hank, Jr., (who had turned five
in May) and I placed two wreaths on Daddy's grave, and Dr.
Henry Lyon offered a devotional. The grave had been moved
two weeks after Daddy's death to a spot better suited for a
future memorial.

At 2:45 P.M. we led the parade from the State Capitol to the
Cramton Bowl, where the big show was going to be held later
that day. Mother, Hank, Jr., Miss Ragland, Mrs. Stone, and I
rode in Daddy's blue Cadillac convertible. I remember waving
and smiling at the cheering crowd for a long time. Behind us
came twenty sections of bands, floats, horses, and celebrities.
There were estimated to be forty to fifty thousand onlookers
lining the parade route.

The three-hour show that night was hosted by Roy Acuff,
who was assisted by Hank Snow and Ernest Tubb. Each
speaker had ten minutes for his or her individual tribute to
Daddy. This historic show featured literally every country music personality of note in the entire industry.

The climax of the weekend was the unveiling of a ten-foot monument to be installed at Daddy's new gravesite. It was made of Georgia marble, designed by Leeburn Eads, a Shriner and a gospel radio show host, and had as its theme Daddy's gospel classic, "I Saw The Light." On the back of the monument was inscribed a poem Mother had written:

❖   ❖   ❖   ❖   ❖

Thank you for all the love you gave me
There could be no one stronger.
Thank you for the many beautiful songs
They will live long and longer.
Thank you for being a wonderful father to Lycrecia
She loved you more than you knew
Thank you for our precious son
And thank God he looks so much like you
And now I can say
There are no words in the dictionary
That can express my love for you
Someday beyond the blue

— Audrey Williams

❖   ❖   ❖   ❖   ❖

That same month Lillie Stone petitioned the court in Montgomery to be named guardian of Hank, Jr.'s portion of his father's estate in Alabama. She argued that, as he was her grandson, with no other legal guardian in Alabama and an estate of his own valued at $2,060.08, she should be overseeing his interests. She was granted the request, required to post a five thousand dollar bond, and ordered to make a financial report every three months.

Less than six months later, on February 26, 1955, she died of a heart attack. She was found dead in her bed by her niece, Marie Harvell. The survivors listed in her obituary were: Irene, Catherine Yvone Stone, two sisters, a brother, and four grandchildren. She had divorced her husband, Bill Stone, the previous fall.

Irene was named the executrix of Lillie's estate as well as the sole heir, and she also succeeded her mother in the administration of Hank, Sr.'s and Hank, Jr.'s Alabama estates.

Cathy Stone, named Antha Belle Jett until she was adopted

by Mrs. Stone, was placed in a foster home and eventually readopted. A petition was filed in her behalf seeking fifty percent of Lillie's estate, but in June it was found that "the Court is of the opinion that the will of Lillian Stone Williams makes no provision for the minor, Catherine Yvone Stone, and is further of the opinion that the adoption of Catherine Yvone Stone, a minor, by Lillian S. Williams after the making of her will does not operate as a revocation of that will in order to permit said minor to inherit a child's share under the Statute of Descent and Distribution or any other provision under the law."

This was the first interpretation of this law in Alabama as applied to an adopted child, but it was not the end of the matter.

Mother was writing and recording as well as touring at this time. And in February 1955, she went out to Hollywood in regard to a movie on Daddy's life. Soon after her return, she recorded her last session with Decca. The soon-to-be-legendary producer Owen Bradley recalls that it was one of those disaster-type things from the beginning. Recording onto tape was very new, and everyone was still learning about the procedures and equipment. Besides, Mother had a bad cold and cough that got worse as the afternoon progressed. None of the songs recorded that day were ever released (nor were the ones from her 1953 session) or even mixed.

Again, however, like her selections in the previous session, there was a heart-rending aspect to her material. For her first song, Mother borrowed Webb Pierce's current hit, "Slowly (I'm Falling More In Love With You)," changed the lyrics, and retitled it "Slowly You Taught Me (What Real Love Can Do)."

"Don't Be Too Quick To Judge" was next. She was responding to the flood of criticism that was to hound her throughout her life, in a plea for understanding. It was written in the spirit of Daddy's Luke the Drifter numbers:

✻   ✻   ✻   ✻   ✻

If you should see me where you think I shouldn't be,
Just give me a smile, don't be too quick to judge me.
Maybe that you don't know my heart's breaking inside,
And maybe you don't see the tears I'm trying to hide.

If you'll just give me a kind word or two,
They would do me more good than idle gossip would do.
So if you should see me where you think I shouldn't be,
Just give me a smile, don't be too quick to judge me.

If you just had the time to listen you'd find
I could tell you a story that would soon change your mind.
Maybe your lucky star's still shining above,
And you've never lost the one that you love.

If you'll just give me a kind word or two,
They would do me more good than idle gossip would do.
So if you should see me where you think I shouldn't be,
Just give me a smile, don't be too quick to judge me.

✻   ✻   ✻   ✻   ✻

MGM signed Mother to a recording contract of her own in early 1955, and she had two sessions for MGM that year. In the first, held about the same time as the final one for Decca, Mother recorded "Making Believe" and "That's All I Want From You"; the fall session consisted of the sentimental favorite "Little Bocephus" and "Windows Of The Past," one of her original compositions.

Meanwhile, in Nashville, I was growing up. I was in the fifth grade when Daddy and Mother divorced and in the sixth grade when Daddy died. I had moved from school to school a lot, and it had left me very shy and withdrawn in the classroom.

My sixth grade teacher, Miss Blackman, told my mother she'd pass me on to the seventh grade if I went to summer school. "But if you want to do her a favor," she said, "let her stay in the sixth grade another year to catch up. One reason she's so bashful and shy is because she's struggling so hard to keep her head above water in school. Let her catch up so she can be more self-confident."

Mother agreed, and I stayed through the sixth grade again, got good grades, and enjoyed school much more. Now I realize that Miss Blackman must have figured that I needed an extra year to help me after everything I had gone through. That year was a turning point for me. I was about to become a teenager, and the new confidence in school boosted my morale.

For my thirteenth birthday in August 1954, Mother treated

me to an elegant party at the glamorous Plantation Club. The girls all wore evening dresses, brought dates, drank champagne, and danced to the music of some of Nashville's best musicians. It was a real dress-up party.

Even though I was starting to enjoy parties and dates, I still loved horses. Beside my horse Trigger, we still had Daddy's horse, High Life, and Hank, Jr., had a miniature Shetland named Dud (a gift from the Hadacol man, Dudley LeBlanc). I didn't ride Trigger much anymore, though, because he was a small pony and I had pretty much outgrown him. Besides, there was really not a good place to ride any of the horses except the backyard since Franklin Road had gotten busier and busier. So Mother decided that it was time to get rid of them all. Daddy and I had had so much fun fooling with the horses, and I hated to see them go.

It wasn't long before I was driving a car and going places, rather than staying home and thinking about riding horses. Mother had bought a white Cadillac El Dorado with a custom-ordered interior of unborn calfskin seats and all the latest in technology — even one of the first car telephones. One time when Lynette was visiting, we drove Mother's car to the drugstore in Melrose, just a few doors down from the Acuff-Rose offices.

When we came out and started home, I backed into whoever was behind me. I was so nervous, all I could do was whistle. Lynette said, "Lycrecia, this is no time to be whistling. You just backed into this man."

I said, "I know it," but I kept on whistling. I couldn't help it. That man probably thought I was just a little rich girl and didn't care, but I always whistled when I was nervous.

That car had a hard life. Mother wrecked it in 1957 on a trip to Montgomery to help set up the second "Hank Williams Memorial Day."

The loyalty and devotion of Daddy's fans had not died as the years passed by, so the Alcazar Temple planned and sponsored another tribute on September 23–24, 1957. The Everly Brothers, Johnny Cash, the Drifting Cowboys, Wilma Lee and Stoney Cooper, Carl Smith, Del Wood, Tillman Franks, Porter Wagoner, Goldie Hill, Rod Brasfield, Autry Inman, Chet

Atkins, Stonewall Jackson, and Jimmy Newman entertained. I got to sing "Jambalaya" and "Your Cheatin' Heart."

The last of the 50s were boom years for Mother. She recorded twice for MGM Records in 1956. "Livin' It up and Havin' a Ball" and "Ain't Nothing' Gonna Be Alright Nohow" were followed by "Let Me Sit Alone and Think" and "Parakeet Polka" about six months later. In August 1957, *Billboard* announced that "Eddie Crandall, former personal manager to Marty Robbins, and Audrey Williams, 'Grand Ole Opry' performer, have opened offices at 2508 Franklin Road to book 'Grand Ole Opry' and other c.&w. talent." The Williams/Crandall agency planned to put together country music packages for road tours and to do promotional and personal management work as well.

In addition to the Eddie Crandall Booking Agency and Audrey Williams Enterprises, Mother's partnership with Eddie Crandall expanded over the next two years to include the Hank Williams Memorial Foundation (which published two Williams family photo albums), the Audrey Williams National Talent Search, and the Audrey Williams Musical Caravan of Stars. Eddie began spending a good deal of time at our house, and it was clear to me that his relationship with Mother had expanded even more to include a romance.

Mother established another important partnership in 1957 with promoter Victor Lewis from Toledo, Ohio. He describes their first enterprise and recalls some of his impressions:

> It was intrigue at first sight. I was intrigued with her star status; she was intrigued with my ideas. She found the idea of a touring country music talent show very appealing. We mounted the show and hit the road rather quickly. The crowds were big, and Audrey was pleased. She was the 'star' of the show, the center of attraction, and she was excited. Actually, the show was more successful than she had expected it to be. Many people were eager to see Mrs. Hank Williams in person. Audrey ran things backstage as well as doing a credible job on stage. I believe that was her first 'being the boss' experience and it appealed to her very much.
>
> Although any change in her personality was imperceptible, I believe that at this early time she may have commenced to change from a sweet, innocent little country girl into Audrey, blonde bombshell of corporate intrigue. Certainly to Audrey's credit was

the fact that she told me, during a long conversation on one of our tours, that what she liked best about our show was the fact that we might help launch a country music career for some boy or girl who would otherwise have to spend the rest of their lives in a factory or behind a counter in some all-night cafe. Actually, we never made any noteworthy talent discoveries, but it wasn't because Audrey did not try. Benevolence was a definite facet of her character, especially if it concerned helping someone get started in Country Music.

I never detected in Audrey the slightest propensity to envy or begrudge. About the good fortune of others, Audrey seemed to feel genuine happiness. She often went out of her way very privately to help others. Once she told me that helping others was a great pleasure and made her feel good about herself. Most generally, Audrey was discreet and anonymous about her gifts of assistance, and she could really assist! When Audrey spoke, people in high places inclined an ear and listened carefully. Her command of influence was awesome. She had about her some potent magic that stemmed in large part from the Hank Williams legend. But not entirely. She had some additional, indefinable appeal of her own.

From the beginning, Vic Lewis's talent show idea spread good will for Mother, and for Daddy's name, too. There was so much positive response from fan mail and local communities that in March 1958 Mother and Victor Lewis jointly announced their organization of a national talent search for the "Country and Western stars of tomorrow." Mother planned to act as mistress of ceremonies and to take the competition from city to city, where local winners would be entered into statewide contests offering one-year recording contracts and other prizes.

The idea for the expanded talent search, she explained, was partially inspired by the flood of fan mail she received from young people who wanted to break into the country music business. She felt that good talent was always needed, so the talent search was a service to the industry as well as an opportunity for talented, ambitious country music hopefuls. "Most important to Audrey," stated the official announcement, "is the fact that she considers her talent search a living public service monument to her late, great husband, the immortal Hank Williams."

Outwardly, Mother appeared happy, energetic, and bursting with creativity. She seemed to be putting the tragic past behind her. Recalling those days, her friend Rena Hailey claims that "it was impossible to know her without loving her."

Rena was a seamstress Mother met in the mid-50s, and she helped Mother with her wardrobe a lot. She remembers Mother was a very beautiful, glamorous-looking woman, but Rena also understood a lot more about what made her act like she did at this point in her life.

That was before that kind of Hollywood glamour came to Nashville. And she was one of a kind. She's the only person I knew that if she was wearing gray, she wore gray all the way through, down to her stockings, lingerie, everything. And she was perhaps one of the cleanest women I have ever known. She was impeccably clean.

Sometimes, though, her glamour was a burden to her. She felt she had an image to maintain as Mrs. Hank Williams, so nobody ever saw her in a sweatshirt or a pair of jeans — no way. But she really was as plain and ordinary and down to earth as she could be. I was privileged to know her mama and daddy, too. There was just not anybody lovelier or more genuinely American than the Sheppards, and much of that had rubbed off on Audrey.

She was a good person. She had a tremendous sense of fair play about her. She wasn't out to do anybody, but, by the same token, they weren't going to do her and get by with it. She was liberated in her own way. She was commanding as well as demanding. She had little patience with people that did not have a quick mind, and she saw far beyond the present situation almost in every instance.

I don't think she did what she did just for Audrey. I think she had a tremendous sense of responsibility to the music profession and was somewhat desperate to see that Crecia and Hank, Jr., would never want for anything.

I think she loved Hank, Sr., very, very deeply. She realized that he was not as strong as she had hoped he would be, and, no matter how hard she had tried, there was no way she could give him her strength. She could stand the pressure of money and fame herself — she was not intimidated by anything or anyone — but I think she was disappointed and guilty that she had perhaps pushed him beyond his own capacity. She loved him as much as he loved her, and she was just so hurt that he was no longer there.

Chapter 13

For in our Son I've Hope

I know Mother wanted to keep Daddy's name alive. She wanted people to always remember what a great songwriter he was. Daddy made the great impression with his songs, but it never hurts for somebody who's still living to keep the memory from dying down. Mother worked at that by herself for the first five years after Daddy died. Then she realized Hank, Jr., could help.

Hank, Jr., was only three and a half years old when Daddy died. We didn't see Daddy but two or three times the last year he was alive, so Hank, Jr., had only very fuzzy memories of him. But he heard a lot about Daddy from the people who came around to see us.

Hank, Jr., described what kind of influence all that had on him in his autobiography *Living Proof.*

See, I was Hank Williams' son, and I lived in Hank Williams' house and Hank Williams' wife was my mother. And let me tell you something — for a little kid, all that is neat . . .

I knew that the people who came to Mother's parties were important in some way . . . and all they could do was tell me how good I was, how smart I was, how much I looked like Daddy, and what a great man he was. . . . I learned to idolize my father. At first, I thought he was like a president or king or something. . . . His memories were all over the place. . . . There were times, I remember, when I was sure that Daddy wasn't dead at all . . .

All the greats in the music industry, they all came to Hank Williams' house, and they all took time out to talk to me and give

137

me a few pointers on the guitar or piano. . . . I knew I'd grow up
to be a singer.

On March 22, 1958, eight-year-old Hank, Jr., made his
stage debut before a packed house at the Nancy Auditorium in
Swainsboro, Georgia, as part of a country music show that
included Mother and me. "The youngster has inherited more
than a smattering of his late father's droll appeal and singing
skill," wrote one newspaper columnist.

After the success of that show, Mother tried to put Hank,
Jr., on the stage whenever she could. She formed the Audrey
Williams Musical Caravan of Stars, a package show that included Mother, Hank, Jr., and me, two "rockabilly" singers
(the Big Bopper and Carl Perkins), and a show and dance
band. Other artists, like Ernest Tubb and Grandpa Jones,
were featured at various times. The caravan shows were scheduled for weekends, holidays, and school vacations so Hank,
Jr., and I would not have to miss school. Hank, Jr., and I used
to sing "Hey, Good-Lookin'" together on the shows.

Mother took time off from her busy schedule in 1958 so we
could drive out to Hollywood, California, sightseeing all the
way. We took the southern route through Texas, New Mexico,
Arizona, and Las Vegas, Nevada. I particularly remember Sunset
Crater in Arizona because I got sick from the lack of oxygen in
the high altitude. Eddie Crandall was with us on that trip.

Mother put a band together in late 1958 that worked for her
pretty consistently over the next year or two. Ken Marvin,
recording star and the original Lonzo of the "Grand Ole Opry"
comedy team Lonzo and Oscar, played guitar and fronted the
band, Howard White played steel, Goober Buchanan was the
bass player/comedian, and Buddy Spicher played the fiddle.
Those musicians came to know Mother well from their day-to-
day contact with her.

Howard White says, "She never interfered with the musicians or tried to tell us how to play or anything. We played
mostly Hank, Sr.'s music. The crowds liked Hank, Jr., and I
thought he did a good job. He was a nice little boy."

Mother asked Buddy Spicher to move to Nashville and work
with her regularly after he filled in for a missing fiddler in
Wheeling, West Virginia. She helped him find a place to stay,
and he remembers a lot about those days in Mother's band.

Most of the time Audrey was strictly business; she was a very hard worker, a go-getter, and a pioneer. If somebody did try to get something over on her, she would say, "They're not going to get this over on ol' Audrow" — she called herself Audrow.

We would have other people on the show, and then after a certain point Audrey would come out with Hank, Jr., and Lycrecia. She didn't interfere or get in our way. Like a good professional, she left the musicians alone, but she had a lot of great musicians in her band. Our main thing was to make sure we backed her up right. But she was never a person who yelled at you or got mad at you if you played the wrong chord. She may not have been the greatest singer in the world, but she was fair and she went over with the audience.

Audrey was a very generous person. Like I said, she was very helpful to me. She was also helpful to literally hundreds of others like me, people who would not have gone anywhere. She more or less financed them or found them work.

We always went first class. We traveled in beautiful Cadillacs, stretch limousines, and stayed in the finest places. A lot of the money she spent was on other people. She was never above us.

I remember I used to be in the habit of bowing my head before I ate and saying a blessing. One time when I first started with her she said, "Hey, Buddy's going to say a blessing." She had me to say the blessing out loud for everybody. I thought that was nice of her.

Goober Buchanan's first tour with Mother was through Mississippi and Louisiana, ending up in Memphis for a Hank Williams memorial show. In addition to playing bass and being the comedian in the group, he also sold books, pictures, albums, and souvenirs. He remembers watching Hank, Jr., during his first performances.

Audrey prompted little Hank — we called him Randall then — on the shows. He played the drums and he wanted to be a rock 'n roller. She had him do the Hank Williams tunes; she would let him do one rock 'n roll song, but the rest she picked. I was so surprised at him. Even as a kid, he seemed to be born to the stage. He never expressed any nervousness or anything; he just came out there and was absolutely natural. Anything he did, he did well. Audrey was very proud of him and the way he went over and the way he imitated Hank's songs. He did sound a lot like Hank. She paid him twenty-five dollars a show, and he was saving up his money to buy a motorcycle. They had the money to buy it, but she wanted him to earn it. She said he would take more care of it then.

Audrey sang Hank's songs, too, and she sang some that she had recorded herself. She went over well. She looked like a movie star on the stage — she was beautiful and had a very good personality in front of a mike. She didn't think she was great or beautiful, though. Once she said to me that she would never marry again because "all a man would want is my money."

I found out she had a weakness for drink, the same as Hank did. Ken Marvin bought her a bottle of scotch on a long trip once, and she got a little too much sitting in the back seat. We had to lock her in her room that night while we went to get something to eat, and when we came back, she had crawled out the bathroom window and was in the car trying to start the motor with the trunk key. That's the only time I saw her get too much to drink.

Both Mother and Daddy had a way of getting around locked doors when they had had too much to drink.

Mother didn't take Hank, Jr., or me on the long three-week tour of Alaska in late January to early February 1959. Eddie Crandall and Victor Lewis made an advance trip up there to promote the show, carrying their advertisements door-to-door in the Eskimo villages. A week or two later, Mother and Vic and the band members, with the addition of bass player/impressionist Benny Williams, flew from Washington to Anchorage, Alaska, to start the tour. The temperature during those cold winter weeks once dropped to forty degrees below zero.

The cold weather didn't keep them from having fun on that trip, though. It was an easy job for the musicians, and they all grew close during the extended tour. "Audrey and Ken Marvin was always having a lot of friendly arguments," recalls Benny Williams, "but she couldn't get nothing on him. I remember we was at a club somewhere in Alaska one night after the show and Ken — we called him Loosh — and Audrey had gotten into an argument. Audrey said, 'Loosh, I guess you know that you can be replaced' and he said, 'I can't think of nobody, my dear, that could be more easily replaced than you.' He was working for her, but he got by with it."

Mother's relationship with Eddie Crandall did not survive much past their return home from Alaska. Benny Williams remembers one time soon after that when Mother got mad at Eddie. "I was driving the car," says Benny, "and I stopped to get gas. Audrey and Eddie was in the back seat and I kept waiting for her to give me some money to pay for the gas. The man was standing there, so I finally said, 'Audrey, you got some money?' She pulled out a fifty dollar bill and threw it up in the front seat, and she said, 'Money is all I got.'"

A minor fling between Mother and steel player Howard White in Alaska hadn't helped matters, and neither did her discovery in late February that Eddie had taken a girl to their Franklin Road office "to listen to some records or something" when she was out of town. She ended it as soon as she got back home. During the time they dated, Mother spent a considerable amount of money on Eddie, buying him a pink Cadillac, expensive clothes, and picking up the tab for most of their entertainment expenses. However, I think Eddie seemed to care genuinely for Mother and was capable of giving as well as taking.

I was developing a romantic relationship of my own at this time. Unlike the rest of my family, I have never enjoyed being in the spotlight. All I have ever wanted was to be a wife and a mother and stay at home and take care of my family. I don't like people paying so much attention to me. There were some parts of traveling and singing before an audience that I liked, but I got tired of it. I don't like having to give little pieces of me out all the time — that's just not me.

But Mother wanted more for me. She wanted me to have all the best things in life that she didn't have. She gave me piano lessons and planned to send me to school in California so I would become a model or an actress.

I met Lamar Morris when I was only fourteen. I went to visit my grandparents in Banks, Alabama, and Lamar, at age seventeen, was playing guitar for Shorty Sullivan over WSFA in Montgomery the summer we met. We dated off and on for several years, and then, on my eighteenth birthday, he gave me an engagement ring. Lamar went to Nashville with me to meet Mother, and she gave me an "L" initial ring for my birthday that I still wear. We were married in June 1960 and moved to Montgomery.

Mother didn't want me to marry Lamar, but not because she didn't like him. She wanted me to marry somebody who was well-off, and Lamar was not well-off. But he was a good man, and money is not everything to me. Mother took to bed sick just before the wedding, and I asked her doctor if I should postpone the wedding. He said, "Absolutely not," and she did fine after that.

From the time of my marriage, Mother concentrated all her energy on Hank, Jr.'s career. She could already see that he seemed to be born to the stage. Even at eleven years old, he was easy and unselfconscious before an audience. As his voice matured, it naturally imitated Daddy's so closely that it could send shivers up a listener's spine. He was not a star in his own right yet; he was only a novelty act. But, as Hank, Jr., later wrote, "Mother knew I was close. So we pushed together." There were many things to worry about, though, he remembered. "Did I sound enough like Daddy on stage? How was Mother doing; was she happy; did she think I was working hard enough? Was I working hard enough?"

Mother's whole thing was keeping Daddy's name alive and being Mrs. Hank Williams and trying to live up to all that. Then with Hank, Jr., I think Mother was afraid that she couldn't live up to producing another star. She wanted Hank, Jr., to be successful for him and for her, too.

In June 1963, the Chancery Court of Davidson County, Tennessee granted a petition filed by Hank, Jr., and Mother to have her appointed his legal guardian in Tennessee. Ten and a half years after Daddy's death, Mother was finally able to enter into legal contracts and agreements for Hank, Jr.

It was about this same time that Buddy Lee, an ex-professional wrestler who was promoting shows in Columbia, South Carolina, began working with Mother and Hank, Jr.

> I told Audrey I'd like to put on a Hank, Jr., show, and I quoted her a price of three hundred dollars. We confirmed the price and the date, and I told her what I had in mind was sort of a tribute to Hank Williams, Sr., featuring his son. She called me later and told me she also sang and would have to drive since Hank, Jr., was only thirteen or fourteen, and that would be an extra hundred and fifty dollars. I said that was fine. Now I had Hank Williams' son and wife. I gave Hank, Jr., and Audrey equal billing with the star

of the package, and we sold out the building. The show was at the Township Auditorium on Taylor Street in Columbia. Hank went over like a million dollars. Audrey did, too. I asked Audrey if she'd like to play some more dates, and she said she would. We bought another major headliner, and we played three dates in three cities. Again, there was a tribute to the late and great Hank Williams.

After the third date Audrey said, "I think I need a little more money, Honey," so it went up to five hundred for Hank. Actually, she was helping without charging. She paid for gas and hotels and, if you knew Audrey, she stayed in the best hotels.

At the time, they were working on a record deal with MGM Records, but MGM wasn't too sure Hank's son could make it. So we decided to do a sixteen city tour to prove that Hank, Jr., would sell. We took him into cities that hadn't had Country Music for ten years. We had a package show with other good acts, and we went from the Carolinas to New England. Immediately following that fall tour in 1963, Hank, Jr., signed a contract with MGM [in December, for three hundred thousand dollars over three years].

Everywhere we went, if we didn't have a sell-out, it was near a sell-out. There was no TV advertising, so we'd barnstorm a city, just go in before the show and put posters up on poles. When the people knew that Hank's wife and son were there, we'd do box office business.

After the sixteen-city tour, I had moved to Boston. Audrey called me there and said they were starting to get a lot of calls to book Hank, Jr., and she wanted me to come to Nashville. I didn't want to make a move because I didn't know Audrey that well, but after the fourth or fifth call, I flew down and we made a deal for me to represent him and promote the dates. Audrey would still manage him, but I'd find the cities to play in and secure the building and do the advertising. I immediately talked her into promoting a Hank Williams, Jr., show. Audrey was a gambler, and she said, "We'll do it." At that time, Hank, Jr., was doing Hank, Sr.'s songs, plus he was writing some.

I was there at every show, selling programs, buttons, pictures. She gave me half of what we sold in merchandise. There were times when she'd perform and times when she'd just come along as an overseer. She was a very sharp businesswoman, and her word was her bond. If she made a deal and there was ten thousand dollars in it, she'd pay the ten thousand dollars. We became real tight because I depended on her and she depended on me.

She was a good friend. If she liked you, she'd give you the shirt off her back.

Buddy started a little booking business of his own in Nashville, apart from his arrangement with Mother and Hank, Jr. By the time he had signed about five acts, she approached him about buying into his booking agency.

"But I don't have an agency, Audrey," Buddy explained.

"Honey," she said, "I know what you're doing, and I'd like to buy into it. How much are you going to charge me?"

"Well," Buddy told her, "you asked me to come down here, and Hank's been a good product. I'm making money with you."

"What'll we call it?" she asked.

"I don't know," said Buddy. "Give me ten minutes . . . Well, how about Aud-Lee?"

"Honey, that's great!" she said. "Now you have to move downtown. I've got room for you in the suites I have at 812 16th Avenue."

"It started moving," recalls Buddy, "and we started signing other acts. This was November 1964 that we formed the agency."

In addition to her efforts regarding Hank, Jr.'s blossoming career as a performer and recording artist and the establishment of the Aud-Lee Agency, Mother was involved in a number of other major projects in the early 60s. She started work on a pool, bathhouse, and Japanese garden at the Franklin Road house, began building a chalet for herself in Gatlinburg (in the Great Smoky Mountains) and a new home for her parents outside of Banks, Alabama, and formed a motion picture company that would eventually turn out three major motion pictures.

While in Alaska, Mother had mentioned to Vic Lewis how much she treasured the kinescope recording of Daddy's appearance on "The Kate Smith Show." When she told him that it was the only filmed record of Daddy in existence, Vic said, "A great light appeared and illuminated a corner of my mind." This conversation led to the formation of Marathon Pictures, Inc.

In July 1963 filming began for the first feature length motion picture ever made in Nashville, *Country Music on Broadway*.

It premiered in November at the Tennessee Theater in Nashville and was filmed in Eastman Color, except for the black and white kinescope of Daddy from the Kate Smith Show. Mother, Hank, Jr., and I were featured in the movie, along with about twenty major country music performers. The highlight of the movie was the scene in which Hank Snow reminisced about his friend, Hank Williams, Sr., and asked Hank, Jr., if he'd like to see a "home movie" (the kinescope) of his late father.

Second Fiddle to a Steel Guitar was released the following year. It starred an even greater array of country music performers, including Minnie Pearl, Webb Pierce, Kitty Wells and Johnny Wright, Lefty Frizzell, Little Jimmy Dickens, Faron Young, Bill Monroe, and many more.

According to Vic Lewis:

Prior to Marathon Pictures, nearly every act in Nashville had resolved never again to appear in a filming venture. Only because of their high regard for Audrey did they make an exception in our case.

During this period when Audrey was held in favor and esteem, she was revered by not only country music folk, but industry generals, business persons and artists of note. She was usually treated majestically, and the snap of her fingers would command instant service. People nearly curtsied in her presence.

She absolutely radiated affluence, authority, and charm. Not only did she have a striking appearance, she always had an aura of energy that overwhelmed friends and adversaries alike.

Vic also adds that Mother insisted on portraying her version of a corporate executive every day at work. He believes that this period was a definite turning point in her life.

There had been talk as far back as 1954 about a movie to be made on Daddy's life, with much guess work about who would play the lead role.

When MGM finally began filming *Your Cheatin' Heart* in Hollywood in spring 1964, George Hamilton was cast in the starring role, Susan Oliver was his co-star, and Red Buttons and Arthur O'Connell were the supporting character actors.

Fifteen-year-old Hank Williams, Jr., had been signed to record Daddy's songs for the soundtrack.

The film premiered in Montgomery on November 5, and the next day, November 6, in Nashville at the Country Music Association convention.

The movie did not show Mother in a very good light, although she "oversaw every foot of the film that was shot during the taking of the movie." She tried to explain to an interviewer in 1973 that "Hank was gone and he could not protect himself, and I did not want the people walking away from that theatre and not liking Hank. I wanted them walking away loving him, as they do today. I am still alive, and I can kind of protect myself. So that's one reason I threw it in the light I did and I could have changed it if I had wanted to because I had all the say-so on it."

Mother also explained her reasons for using Hank, Jr.'s voice on the soundtrack instead of the original recordings.

> [At the time] I was trying to build another Hank, my son, Hank, Jr. Originally, we had planned for Hank, Jr., to play his dad's part as a boy, but by the time we did the movie, Hank, Jr., was so grown up we couldn't do that, so I had to go about it from another angle in order to get Hank, Jr., in the picture. Everybody I talked to said this fifteen-year-old boy cannot do the soundtrack.
>
> So I flew back to Nashville, took Hank, Jr., into a recording studio and put down four or five of his dad's songs, and flew back to L.A. with them. I called up the head guy out there and I said, "I've got something I want you to listen to." I played the demo, and after a couple of songs he said, "Regardless of who that is, he's got to do the soundtrack." I said, "This is my son that I've been trying to tell you people about."

I don't know why Mother presented the movie as she did, because not only did she come off badly, but the story itself was not true to the way things really happened. Wesley Rose had warned her that she was making a mistake and would be sorry to have to live with the results, but she was seemingly blind to the damage that she was doing to herself. And her drinking was beginning to become more of a problem.

Before I married and moved to Montgomery, Mother was just drinking socially. Sometimes she might have too much, but it wasn't something she did often. When Lamar and I moved back to Nashville in the summer of 1963, I noticed that she was drinking on a more regular basis. She would get drunk more often than she used to, and it would take her about a day to sleep it off.

We moved back because Mother told Lamar she'd help him get started with a music career. She had parties out by the pool and invited some of the artists and promotion men for Lamar to get acquainted with. But at a party, Mother would always drink too much, and you can't conduct business and drink. Consequently, she never did help Lamar in the way she had planned.

About that time she'd decided to put Hank, Jr., on the road full-time. She asked Lamar to help her get a band together for Hank, Jr. That was it as far as her doing anything for Lamar. He brought the bass player Charlie Norrell, and drummer Larry Joe Williams from Alabama, and got the piano man Bill Aikins, and they formed the Cheatin' Hearts, Hank, Jr.'s first regular band.

Also at this time, little by little, Mother started dating younger men. Then she began to bring them home to live out in the apartment over the garage. She would buy them clothes and gifts.

Hank, Jr., had a hard time with Mother bringing these young men home. I think boys look up to their mothers and feel that they are never supposed to do anything wrong. It bothered me, too, for Mother to do that, especially since I was in my twenties and so were they. But I think it was more devastating to Hank, Jr.

I was too young at the time to understand what Mother was going through, being alone and needing the emotional strength of someone else. I don't think she really cared that much about the young men she dated. It was just the fact that even though she was only in her late 30s, she felt like she was getting old. I guess it made her feel younger, even though she knew that they were there because she was supporting them. Some of them wanted to be singers, so she was trying to help them get started in a career, but at the same time she was romantically involved with them.

And I think she did a lot of that just so people would talk

about her, just so she could be punished a little bit more and could make people think the worst of her because she didn't have any self-esteem.

Vic Lewis thinks Mother wanted to remarry, but she had too much to lose because her divorce agreement would cut off her royalties should she remarry. "Her social life was misunderstood by many who perceived Audrey as a party girl, a substance abuser, or a lonely, frustrated widow," he says.

Mother's most serious affair was with a young man named Bob Eddings. She met him in 1964 while he was a student at the Air Force Academy in Denver, and he moved to Nashville in 1965 and was in and out of her house until 1967. Although they parted ways, they remained friends.

Mother met her friend and secretary Erma Williams in 1964, about the time she began dating Bob Eddings. Erma lived in Houston, and sometimes Mother would fly into Houston and Erma would pick her up at the airport and drive her up to Orange, Texas, to see Bob.

"She was very serious about Bob Eddings," states Erma. "He was probably the only man she would have considered marrying. He moved to Nashville, and things were going great, but yet they would have their arguments. I think at one time she might have married him, but it scared her when it got right down to it, and I think it scared Bob, too. I think he truly cared for her, but their wills clashed. He did not want to become Mr. Audrey Williams and lose control over his own life."

In some ways Mother had the same kind of problem with Hank, Jr., and me. She couldn't find the right amount of love to give along with the right amount of control. She was not what you would call motherly, but under all that businesswoman strength she cared very much for us. I know she wanted both of us to be independent and to have the gumption to get up and do what needed to be done.

Erma Williams, who was not any kin to us, has helped me figure out why Mother seemed the way she did to so many people, especially when it came to Hank, Jr.

At the time I first met Audrey, Hank, Jr., was still living at home. He was a kid, a very mature kid intellectually. He loved his mother, he wanted to be obedient, and yet he was at that stage when he also wanted to find his own identity and be himself.

I'm sure Hank, Jr., was disappointed that he didn't have the kind of mother who attended PTA meetings and was there making cookies when he got home. And when he was a teenager, there were things she did that embarrassed him.

I think she was so afraid that if she came over with too much warmth for Hank, Jr., he would see it as a weakness. She realized her strength had been what Hank, Sr., had depended on. I think when it came right down to it, she was afraid to really reveal herself to either one of her children, because if she had, she would be losing some control. She felt she had to be strong for her children's sake.

And Audrey was as proud of Lycrecia as she was of Hank, Jr. She used to tell me what a good wife Lycrecia was and what a good little mother. So many times she'd say, "Lamar doesn't know how lucky he is to be married to my daughter."

Audrey did not realize that her love could be such a smothering love. She didn't want just part of your time, she wanted it all. It was like, "If you love me, you will do this for me," and "If you love me, you won't do this to me."

Besides her children, there was only one thing that was more important to Audrey than being Mrs. Hank Williams, and that was being loved. She never really felt like she was loved. It was almost as though if you loved Audrey, you were in a constant state of proving it to her.

In her book, *Co-Dependency/Misunderstood and Mistreated,* Anne Wilson Schaef describes the characteristics of co-dependents. They are supreme controllers, she states, because they fear abandonment and, therefore, need to be involved in every aspect of the lives of their "significant others." To them, not to be involved equals abandonment. They try to possess other people because they cannot really believe that others would want them around unless forced to do so. To co-dependents, everything is personalized. They believe that whatever happens is a result of what they have or haven't done, and that they can and should be able to fix anything.

The main goal in life for co-dependents is to please others, and when they cannot, they believe they are personal failures. Since their self-esteem is low, 'they feel the need to make themselves indispensible. They desperately need to be needed.

It is painful to see how Mother's life exemplified these qualities. Of course, nobody understood this at the time.

In April 1964 Mother filed a petition in the Montgomery County courts to have herself declared Hank, Jr.'s Alabama guardian. She argued that she was already his legal guardian in Tennessee and that Irene Smith (Hank, Sr.'s sister), Hank, Jr.'s guardian in Alabama, was a resident of Texas, had had no personal contact with Hank, Jr., for years, and was receiving large annual fees for being his guardian. Irene petitioned for the suit to be dismised based on her past record of efficiency and the increased value of the estate. In April of the following year, Irene's request for dismissal was granted, so Mother lost her bid to be Hank, Jr.'s Alabama guardian.

Mother decided that Hank, Jr., needed a touring bus. She bought a used two-level Scenic Cruiser from the Trailways Company in the summer of 1964 and had the inside converted into traveling and living quarters for road trips. So much of the life Mother, Hank, Jr., and my husband Lamar lived in the mid-60's was either on that bus or getting on and off to play tour dates.

Trucker Marvin Smythia (Smitty) was hired to drive the bus and make sure it was kept in good running order.

"I went over and talked to Audrey," recalls Smitty, "and she said, 'I'm afraid of truck drivers. They're supposed to be bad men.'

"I told her, 'Well, I'm not big enough to be bad.'

"She said, 'O.K., I'll tell you what we'll do. You go to work with us, and if we like you after a month, we'll keep you and if you like us, you'll stay.'

"So I went to work for her. I went over to the house on Franklin Road, and she gave me the keys to the bus and said, 'Now it's yours.' She warned me that it broke down all the time, and she wanted it ready to go at any time. I told her all it would take was time and money."

That very night Smitty started driving, and his recollections describe touring and Mother pretty well.

I got on the bus that night, and I had never met any of them besides Audrey. Hank, Jr., had an old cannon in the front yard. I was sitting on the bus by myself—it was about eleven at night— and all at once, that cannon went off and here comes everybody to the bus. It scared me to death. There was Lamar Morris, Hank's brother-in-law, Charlie Norrell, Larry Joe Williams, and Bill Aikins.

It wasn't long before I blew the engine up at the New York line. Audrey asked me what I wanted to do with it, and I told her I wanted to bring it back to Nashville. She told me to get a wrecker and do whatever I wanted. She wasn't on the bus at the time, but the guys got cars and went on with the tour. After they brought the bus back to Nashville, I took a truck two-speed axle, turned it upside down backwards and put it in. Also a 238 Detroit engine and a five-speed puller overdrive transmission. There was an old saying, "it would outrun a telephone call," and it would. There hasn't been a bus on the road would run that fast. Still not. It topped out at 130 miles per hour. That's the way they wanted to ride. The patrol caught me in Virginia once at one twenty-eight. I brought in tickets by the handful, and they paid them.

We thought the world of Audrey, my wife Dot and I. She was as truthful with us as the old saying, "either take your raincoat or you're going to get wet." There's never been a better singer than Hank Williams, but as far as a person to work for, there's never been a better person than Audrey.

Of course, she always stayed in the best places she could find. Even if I was dirty and greasy, she'd just say, "Where I go, you can go."

My only instructions were "be there on time" and "no women on the bus." She also told me I didn't have to unload equipment or run errands. I was only supposed to look after the bus and drive it. Of course, I did help them load and unload. The only time she ever got onto me, and Bob Eddings, too, was once in a little place in southwest Texas when Hank went off to a gun shop and Bob and I went on back to the motel. She told us, "If you go out with Hank, Jr., you're supposed to come back with Hank, Jr."

Smitty and Dot became good friends with all the boys in the band. We all had cook-outs and went hunting and fishing to- gether. Hank, Jr., was always with us, too. I sure miss those good times.

Tommy Cash, a singer and the brother of Country Music legend Johnny Cash, signed with Aud-Lee and started riding

Hank, Jr.'s bus in 1965. He remembers that Mother was always around.

> She was at the shows, she was at the hotel, she was on the bus, she was everywhere. She insisted on the sound being good and everyone dressing sharp. She was always brushing lint off of everyone or straightening your shirt collar.
>
> She used to tell me, "Now, Tommy, I don't want you to keep Hank, Jr., up all night playing cards. He needs his rest, and I don't want you all drinking," but, of course, we didn't pay much attention to her. We drank a lot and played poker, sometimes for big money. Audrey would find out about it, and she'd say, "Please don't do that with Hank, Jr.," and we'd say, "But, Audrey, he's the one that calls us up!" She'd say, "Well then, just try to keep it to a minimum. We've got to do the shows." She was very aware of everything that was going on. You couldn't keep anything from her.
>
> When the show was over, she'd always congratulate Hank, Jr., on doing a good job and tell him how much she appreciated him and how much the audience loved him. She did that for all of us. But when you did a bad show, she'd tell you that, too.
>
> Many times I'd look over and see her watching Hank, Jr. I remember one night I caught her looking at him like she stood in awe of him. Her eyes were partly closed, and her head was back. I think she knew there couldn't be another Hank Williams, but that Hank, Jr., could be just as big in a different way.

Once Hank, Jr., wrote a song, "Standing in the Shadows," while riding on the bus. When he showed it to Mother, she smiled, and in his autobiography, *Living Proof,* he remembered that "the front section of the bus lit up with that smile." As he watched her, "the smile changed into sort of a half frown, and . . . When she finished reading the song and started to hand me back the paper, I realized that she was crying and that everything had gotten very quiet on the bus."

CHAPTER 14

Where Do I Go from Here?

Sometimes you can look back on a person's life or at when things happened, and you can see there was a time when too much came at a person for them to handle — even if they were in very good shape to start with. I think that's about the way it was with Mother during 1966 and the early part of 1967 — and she was no longer in very good shape. As her problems increased, so did her drinking.

In the spring of 1966, Marathon Pictures was dissolved over a conflict between Mother and Vic Lewis regarding the filming of a full-length gospel movie, *Sing a Song for Heaven's Sake*. The company was having financial difficulties, and Mother's behavior was getting more unpredictable. In the breakup, Mother met two attorneys who would figure significantly in her life over the next several years: James Neal, later an internationally known criminal lawyer, and an Illinois attorney named Joe Williamson.

About the same time, Mother formed a new corporation, the Ly-Rann Music Publishing Company. The name of the company was formed from my name and Randall's. Ly-Rann was set up to self-publish the songs Hank, Jr., was beginning to write, like the autobiographical "Standing in the Shadows," but Mother soon added other writers to build up Ly-Rann's catalog of songs. First she took on Jack Sanders to run the new publishing company. Then, in early 1966, she hired songwriter/artist Murv Shiner. Also in 1966, she hired Mack Vickery, who went on to become a very successful songwriter.

Mack remembers Mother as "just real down-home, Alabama friendly," and at the same time, "lonely, even with all those people around. . . . She had a great sense of humor. She told me one time, 'Dahling, the only thing an old man can bring me is a note from a young man.'"

Mack has many memories of working with Mother.

We didn't write much in the office, but Audrey had an apartment up over the breezeway and garage and we used it kind of like a music room. I didn't live there, but I spent a lot of time out there and people would come over. Waylon used to, back in that era, and Jerry Lee, Johnny Cash, and, of course, Hank was there. Audrey liked to have a lot of friends around.

Audrey was a good-hearted person and probably one of the best friends I ever had. I never had a contract with her. I never needed one. Her word was good. She would always take time to listen. People would just wander off the street, and when nobody else would see them, Audrey would say, "Well, come on in, Dahling."

One of the things that stands out in my mind was an old ragged-looking fellow that wanted somebody to listen to his song. Audrey was getting ready to leave, and she said, "Well, all right, Dahling. Come on, I'll listen to it." The song wasn't any good, but she was nice to him and said she just couldn't use it.

One time a bunch of us were out at the house. We had partied all night, and it was about ten in the morning and these people came up and knocked on the door. Audrey asked me to see who it was, and there were some tourists there. I told her, and she went and talked to them and said that the place was really not open to the public, but "Y'all go on and take a look and make yourselves at home."

Sonny Throckmorton, another of Nashville's most respected songwriters, succeeded Murv Shiner as Ly-Rann's chief song-plugger in early 1967.

I had heard all these horror stories about Audrey, but I found her to be everything opposite of what I had heard. She was really a great lady. I always thought the world of Audrey and I would go to bat for her anytime and anyplace. She holds a dear spot in my heart.

Mainly I did what I needed to do, and she did her thing. She was really a neat boss. She would leave me alone except once a day she'd call and if I wasn't there, she'd get very upset. I said, "Audrey, I can't be there and pitch songs, too" and she said, "Honey, I believe I'd rather have you there than pitching songs." When she wanted to talk to you, she wanted to talk to you right then.

Ninety-nine percent of the time she was a blonde, but every once in awhile she'd come in with black hair and this black-haired person was a hard-nosed businesswoman. You just stayed out of her way those days. It only happened once or twice while I was there. The first time it caught me by surprise, but the second time I just laid back and watched it. She'd start at the front and chew her way all through the building. All the stuff that had been troubling her, she'd get it off her chest that day.

I signed Johnny McRae up that year but, unfortunately, I wasn't that good of a songplugger. I tried, but I've got to say that during that time I didn't do her as much good as she did me.

Throughout these years, Mother was spending money hand-over-fist. Her investments in Marathon Pictures, the chalet in Gatlinburg, her parents' new home, the pool and Japanese bathhouse, and, especially, Hank, Jr.'s career were staggering. Also, there were her operating costs for Aud-Lee and Ly-Rann, her travel, and domestic and personal expenses. She was buying extravagant things like a car for Hank, Jr., custom-designed by Nudie, the Hollywood tailor. It was country music's first "Silver Dollar Car," and it was decorated with 574 silver dollars inlaid into the interior, 37 pistols, horseshoes, silver horses, and a real Western saddle.

That same year (1966) when she began to see Hank, Jr., start to show the signs of teenage rebellion, she took steps that she hoped would keep him close to her. She set in motion the plans to add an entire wing, including a ballroom, jacuzzi, and exercise room, to the Franklin Road house for Hank, Jr., although he never showed any interest in it. She wound up spending about three hundred thousand dollars to do this.

Meanwhile, Mother's heavy drinking and two decades of inner turmoil had begun to show their effects. The *Billboard* of March 4, 1967, reported that "Audrey Williams was recently released from the hospital following an extended stay for treatment of a stomach ailment." Mother had entered Miller's Clinic complaining of external bleeding and not being able to keep anything on her stomach. The doctors performed exploratory surgery and found a blood vessel bleeding into her stomach. They removed part of her stomach, and her intestines were rerouted. From this point on, she never felt really healthy again for the rest of her life.

Opry star Jean Shepard remembers receiving a call from Mother from the hospital at the time of the operation. Jean had opened a lot of shows for Hank, Jr., in the mid-60s, and she still feels a deep love for both Mother and him.

I was doing a TV show in Nashville called the "Opry Matinee" one afternoon, and after I got off they paged me to the phone and it was Audrey. I hadn't talked to her in five or six months. I said, "You heifer, where're you at?" and she started crying and said she was in the hospital and would I come to see her. It was a Friday and we had to do the Friday night Opry, so I didn't even go home and change clothes because I felt it was important that I go and see her.

I walked in and we talked for awhile, and I asked her if Hank, Jr., had been by, and she started crying and said, "No." She had been there four or five days, and he hadn't called or anything. I was hurt for her and furious at Hank, Jr., because I felt he was being an inconsiderate brat.

That night, around the Opry, I asked if anybody had seen Hank, Jr., and when I got home, I started making phone calls and leaving word around at different places for him to call me. Well, he called me Saturday afternoon, and I told him his mother was in the hospital and he should go see her. I said, "Hank, Jr., that is your mother. The least you can do is call her." I really ran him over the coals.

The next day I called Audrey, and she asked me did I talk to Hank, Jr., and I asked why, and she said he had called and she thought I might have had something to do with it. I said it didn't matter as long as he had called. I don't care what the big rift was that later developed between them. I know that deep down Hank, Jr., loved his mother. I think her goal was to keep the name of Hank, Sr., alive until Hank, Jr., could come into his own. She once told me, "I know a lot of people don't like me, but I'll still make my son into a star."

A lot of times riding along on the bus, she'd maybe be sitting across the aisle from me and she'd be very quiet, and you could

just tell by the look on her face that there was a sadness about
her — like, "It's me against the world."

Sometime during 1966, the idea was planted in Hank, Jr.'s
mind that it would be to his best interests to have himself declared of age, or emancipated, on his eighteenth birthday, in
May 1967. Then he could make his own business and professional decisions without Mother. The idea was presented to
Mother as necessary to help with problems out on the road,
but Mother was not stupid. She knew that more than just the
legal right to sign checks was involved, and she was not ready
to turn him out unprotected into the world at large.

During this time when Mother was not well, there were periods when she didn't work at all, and besides, she was very
involved at the time in building onto the house. The Aud-Lee
Agency hired Dolores Smiley in 1966 to straighten out the
mess at the office. Dolores traveled with the road show as a
female vocalist and handled the money; back at the office, she
helped Buddy sell the dates, did the collecting, plus all of the
secretarial work. She watched the way Hank, Jr., was being
pushed to emancipation.

People started telling Hank Jr., "You need to get emancipated,
you need to handle your own affairs, you're old enough." Audrey
didn't want the emancipation in one respect, because she would
lose control of the money and Hank, Jr., but she would say to me
in conversation, "I guess maybe it's a good thing because I'm not
well." Then she'd say she didn't want it because he was only eighteen and there were people trying to contol him. It was very con-
fusing.

I personally don't believe that Audrey ever did anything with an
ulterior motive. I think everything she did was to build Hank, Jr.,
and keep Hank Williams' name alive. She spent a huge amount of
money on him in so many ways. She was building the house for
him, but he didn't want any part of it, and he went and got an
apartment. I definitely think people were convincing him that she
was not looking after his best interests, and she was taking his
money and not doing right by him.

When Audrey wasn't drinking, she was fine, but when she was
drinking, she was very difficult. Most of the time when I was
around her, though, she was straight. She had a lot of clout with

certain things because of her money and her name, but she could drive people crazy sometimes. She was very, very impatient, and if she couldn't do any good over the telephone, she'd get on an airplane and go to New York or California and do whatever she had to do.

Audrey knew her whole world was about to fall apart. That's what it boiled down to. She knew that everybody was trying to get control of Hank, Jr., away from her, and he at that time had become convinced that that's what he should do. She held her head up high through it all, though, she truly did. It's always been the same old story in the music business. People get to the point where they think they did it all themselves, and nobody else is to get any credit for anything. That mostly comes from the influence of other people.

To the best of my recollection, Audrey was told that if she wouldn't fight the emancipation, she wouldn't be prosecuted for a substantial amount of Hank, Jr.'s money that was unaccounted for. She could very well have gone to jail. Hank, Jr., wouldn't have known all that if the lawyers hadn't told him. He was so adamant about it, but he was just a kid who had been overly protected and had never had any life of his own, so to speak.

On May 26, 1967, Hank, Jr.'s eighteenth birthday, he was granted the "removal of the disability of minority." He consented to his mother's final accounting of his affairs and discharged her from any and all obligations.

Mother broke off her relationship with Bob Eddings around this same time. She began to go to the chalet in Gatlinburg and to night spots around Nashville with her friend Erma Williams on a pretty regular basis. Erma was a teacher, and she recalls spending a lot of time with Mother on the weekends and whenever school was out.

Audrey would say, "Come on over and stay with me." I would drive across town, and a lot of times we'd go to Gatlinburg. It was always a beautiful drive, and Gatlinburg at the time was not so commercial. Sometimes we'd stop and get a small bottle of Lancer's wine and go back to the chalet, make a fire, and just relax. Audrey was a good cook. She could not prepare a variety of things, but she had her specialties, and what she did cook was good and she enjoyed doing it.

Usually Audrey wanted to go over to the ski lodge, which was next to the chalet. There was always a big, roaring fire and a glass-enclosed area where you could sit and watch the skiers. I never saw Audrey get wild drunk in Gatlinburg ever. She'd have a drink or two, maybe three or four, but it was over a period of time because we'd sit there and talk. Sometimes there would be a little band, and we'd dance. Those are some of the best memories I have of Audrey.

Lots of times we'd go to Printer's Alley and eat where all the music business people hung out. Very often Audrey would invite the entire table to come back home with us. Generally, she paid for all the partying, but not always. People would come over when we were at a club, and Audrey'd say, "Have a drink. What do y'all want to drink?" Everybody would have a drink or two and then leave, and the bill would come to Audrey. That used to make me furious, but she really didn't seem to mind. It was almost as if she needed the attention, and if she had to pay for it, she was willing. To her, money was just something to be used. She would get concerned over spending small amounts. She'd compare the prices on two cans of beans, for instance, but the big money — she never gave it a thought. I was with her one night when someone needed a loan of ten thousand dollars, which she made and never got back.

One night we were somewhere and a couple of guys were really getting obnoxious. They wouldn't go away. Suddenly she leaned over and put her hand on my knee and said, "Oh dahling, let's go home, I just can't keep my hands off of you another minute!" It was all I could do to keep a straight face. One man excused himself, and shortly the other one did, too. We laughed about that for years. She was quick and had a great sense of humor, even about herself.

Audrey was not a pleasant drunk. Her thinking would become totally irrational, and she could be verbally and even violently abusive, like the time she got mad at Bob Eddings and shot the windows out of his car.

But at times, she was a very frightened little girl, especially where her children were concerned. She just couldn't understand why Hank, Jr., couldn't see how much she loved him and that all of what she was trying to do was for his own good. She felt this way about it: "I have to do it. He may not thank me now, but he will someday."

People would be "friends" to Audrey's face, and yet they would talk about her behind her back. I saw that. She was hurt a lot because she believed that these people loved her. Some of them were real users, and Audrey couldn't say no.

I remember one night in particular when Audrey and I were at Boots Randolph's place in Printer's Alley with several people. Audrey was sitting by me, and I was squeezed into the corner. Audrey's lawyer, Joe Williamson, was sitting on her other side and was saying things like 'Oh Audrey, Sweetheart!" while he was kissing her hand and arm. She was drunk and didn't notice him sliding her beautiful diamond "A" ring off her finger while he was fawning over her.

I noticed it, though, so I said, "Audrey, where's your ring?" and she began to cry because she thought she had lost it. I leaned over and looked Joe in the eye and said, "Joe, don't you think you can find it? Maybe in these plants."

Joe knew that I knew what he had done because of the way I looked at him, and suddenly the ring was there. What a cute little trick!

The office situation at Aud-Lee was becoming very volatile by this time. Mother was being more influenced by accountant Ed Neely and Joe Williamson. Ed Neely handled Mother's account books, so he knew better than anybody what she was doing with her money. Nevertheless, he caused a lot of serious trouble by neglecting to pay the taxes she owed the IRS year after year. As for Joe Williamson, he was the type who was constantly urging Mother to "have another drink, Honey," according to Erma. Buddy Lee didn't like the way things were going and was beginning to think of pulling out of Aud-Lee and starting his own agency.

In October 1967 shooting was due to begin on *A Time To Sing*, Hank, Jr.'s first feature film under a new contract with MGM. When Mother and Hank, Jr., left for Hollywood, Hank, Jr., wanted to take his steady girlfriend, Sharon Martin, to California with him, but Mother wouldn't allow it. I don't think Mother disliked Sharon. She just believed Hank, Jr., would be ruining his life by closing off his options so young. It really devastated her when he sneaked out of Hollywood, flew home, and married Sharon on November 6. They were both eighteen, but Hank, Jr.'s recent emancipation had given him the legal ability to marry without a parent's consent.

Jean Sopha, who worked for Aud-Lee at that time, says Hank, Jr., threatened not to finish the movie, but Buddy Lee talked him into going back.

Hank, Jr.'s marriage also brought out the conflict between Mother and Miss Ragland. There was a natural jealousy between them in that Miss Ragland had practically raised Hank, Jr., and she thought of him as her own child. She always saw that he got whatever he wanted, and she had a lot to say about Mother's weaknesses to Hank, Jr.

For several years, Mother had been taking a sedative called Equinil to calm her nerves and help her sleep, and she had begun to take more than she should. When she was doing that and drinking, she wasn't the same Audrey. She did not make good judgments about people and business anymore. She listened to the wrong people, usually the people who were taking her out every night — Ed Neely and Joe Williamson.

Buddy Lee says, "They were afraid that Audrey was going to lose Hank, Jr., because he was on his own, so they convinced her to have a contract drawn up where the attorney would get twenty-five percent of Hank, Jr., the accountant would get twenty-five percent, Audrey would get twenty-five percent, and Hank, Jr., himself would get twenty-five percent. No artist is going to live with that arrangement, but I didn't say anything to Hank. He figured it out for himself. He didn't want to sign the contract, and that was the first time I saw Audrey get really mad at him."

I don't blame Hank, Jr., for not wanting to sign. Mother would have ruined him. She would have lost money, Hank, Jr., would have lost money, and those men would have owned him. By then she just wasn't thinking right most of the time.

Hank, Jr., was so mad that he granted *Billboard*'s Bill Williams an interview and revealed his decision that Mother would no longer retain any booking or management rights over him. "Buddy Lee now will handle all of my affairs, and my mother will have no connection with the agency," he told the reporter. The article appeared in the January 27, 1968, *Billboard* under the heading, "Audrey Williams To Exit Aud-Lee."

"She didn't know anything about it until someone called her and told her to read the latest issue of *Billboard*," recalls Jean Sopha. She came out and wanted to know if we had gotten it, and I gave it to her. That's how she found out. She was devastated. I kept waiting and waiting for her to come out of her office, but she didn't. I really thought she had killed herself. I was scared to go in there. Finally, a couple of hours later, I got up the nerve to crack the door, and she wasn't there. There was another exit door from her office into the hallway, and she had left and gone to Gatlinburg.

When Hank, Jr., pulled out on Mother, she must have felt like everything was falling in on her. But she acted as if nothing really had happened. Jean Sopha says it was very strange because they were all still in the same office together after Hank, Jr.'s decision, it was "business as usual." That sounds like the way Mother acted when she came home after her first husband left her.

In the summer, Buddy Lee, Hank, Jr., and Jean moved to an office across the hall, and Erma came to work for Mother.

In the background of all Mother's drinking and health problems, the house and business expenses, Hank, Jr.'s marriage and emancipation, and finally having him leave her as manager — behind all that Mother had been going through a tangled set of legal suits and proceedings for a year and a half in Alabama.

It had all begun back in September of 1966 when Mother and Hank, Jr., filed a complaint in Montgomery's federal court trying to secure Daddy's business records and personal effects. The defendants named in the action were Irene Smith, the executrix of Daddy's Alabama estate as well as Hank, Jr.'s Alabama guardian, and her attorney, Robert Stewart. This suit expanded in later charges and petitions to include Acuff-Rose as a defendant for entering into a contract with Irene to sell the copyright renewals to Daddy's song catalog for only twenty-five thousand dollars.

The three-way legal battle began on September 18, 1967, in Montgomery, Alabama. Eight lawyers represented the three parties — Mother and Hank, Jr., Irene Smith, and Acuff-Rose — in their fight to determine whose choice it was to assign copyright renewals that would not even go into effect for a dozen years or more.

Most of the Nashville music community sided with Acuff-Rose in the dispute, so Mother's attorneys went to New York to find their own expert witnesses. They all testified that the copyrights had been sold at way below their value.

Only one of Mother's many "friends" came through for her down in Montgomery: Sam Phillips of Memphis, Tennessee, founder of Sun Records and the first to record Elvis Presley and Jerry Lee Lewis. Sam dropped whatever else was on his schedule and went to Montgomery. In the courtroom he was questioned about the value of Daddy's songs.

"One of the attorneys asked me, 'Mr. Phillips, what would you give for the renewal rights on this catalog? What is the minimum you would give?'

"I said, 'Well, Your Honor, before I left Memphis, Tennessee, and drove to Nashville, thinking the trial was there, as busy as I was, I made provisions with the bank to have a half a million dollars ready if it was necessary.' I was putting my money where my mouth was. I didn't have an understanding with Audrey Williams or anything else, I was talking about buying something on the open market."

Mother was given a tough time when she took the witness stand. After estimating that she had spent over three hundred and fifty thousand dollars during the previous three years launching Hank, Jr.'s career, Mother was grilled regarding what she had done with the approximately one and a half million dollars she had received since 1952, personally and for her son. The opposition lawyers charged that the guardianship accounting of funds in Tennessee had shown a shortage of several hundred thousand dollars.

"What you're really looking out for is Audrey Williams," they challenged. "Isn't that right?"

"I'm afraid not," was Mother's reply.

The charges continued, and she admitted to them all: yes, she would lose the royalties if she ever remarried; yes, she had serious problems with the IRS; yes, it was true that she didn't have a "red, copper cent" at the time her guardianship was terminated.

When Robert Stewart asked her what provisions she had made for her son out of all that money, she replied, "I suppose, building his career."

When the time finally came for Mother to speak on her own behalf, she had some very interesting things to say. Acuff-Rose had not done more than any other publisher would have done in promoting Hank's songs, she argued, and, in fact, she and her son had done at least as much to promote the Williams music through their public appearances and performances. "Hank, Jr., doesn't walk on the stage that he doesn't sing mostly his dad's songs," Mother said, and she also mentioned that she had organized a band herself after Hank's death and "talked about Hank's songs every time I went on stage."

On January 30, 1968, only days after Hank, Jr.'s interview was published in *Billboard* magazine, Montgomery Circuit Court Judge Richard Emmet ruled that the contract was in the best interests of Hank, Jr. Acuff-Rose would retain the renewal rights. It was another crushing blow to Mother.

The Montgomery Circuit Court ruling represented a much deeper issue to Mother than who was to retain the publishing rights to Daddy's copyright renewals or even how much money those renewals were worth. What really hurt was the devaluation of the role she had played in keeping Daddy's name and music alive. She had devoted the last fifteen years of her life to those goals, and now the courts had essentially declared her efforts insignificant.

It had also hurt to see how many of her so-called friends had turned away when she needed them the most. Her relationship with Sam Phillips was strengthened, but her faith in the entire Nashville music establishment was permanently shaken. Mother was actually a very private person, and it had always been difficult for her to ask for help or to have her personal problems aired in public. The more than twenty years she had spent as a public figure had hardened her only on the outside. She suffered greatly from the humiliation of the trial and the disregard she felt from her music business peers.

According to both Erma Williams and Sam Phillips, after early 1968, Mother never was the same again.

"Hank, Sr.'s pattern of life was one of the things that really disturbed Audrey deep down," explains Sam. "But she never thought Hank's pattern of life was happening to her. And it wasn't for many years. It was such a gradual thing that she didn't recognize the problem. But that's what the booze and pills do to your mind. Then when you sober up, the little problems become so gigantic. Audrey began to believe all the bad things that were being said about her and she never got around to a turnaround.

"I've never known anyone who was as villified as Audrey. She's been accused of every damn thing — I don't know of anything you can catalog that she hasn't been accused of. And still I didn't have a better friend, there wasn't anybody I had more respect for, despite her faults."

Mother did not realize that her years of struggling to control Daddy's drinking had instilled in her the need to control everything and everyone in her life or else consider herself a failure. This need to control at all costs had created a smothering, dependent type of relationship between her and Hank, Jr. . . . and at the same time, because it consumed so much of her energy, it had left little time for her to just "be there" for her children. The effect of all this on Hank, Jr., was to slowly breed resentment and anger for Mother. An expert explains that co-dependents "live within this dualism: I did not do anything to deserve this and I brought it on myself." So not only did Mother feel betrayed, guilt began to dominate her life, guilt for the things she had done, and those she hadn't.

In some ways it seems like Mother needed to punish herself because she felt it was her fault that Daddy had died like he did. I think she felt that if she had just stuck it out a little longer — if she hadn't left him — he wouldn't have drank so bad, or he wouldn't have done this and that, and he wouldn't have died. As she got older, Mother became more and more self-destructive. It seemed like she would just go out and do or say things that she knew were going to make people talk about her or think bad about her. It was like she felt she didn't want anybody thinking anything good about her.

CHAPTER 15

I'm So Lonesome I Could Cry

There is hardly anything good to tell about the last eight years of my Mother's life. It was like watching her go down the same road with drinking and pills that Daddy had traveled, only it took her a lot longer.

Mother managed to keep up her business and social efforts to some degree, and she tried to pull herself together after the court decision cut her off from any control over the copyright renewals on Daddy's songs.

When Hank, Jr., and Buddy Lee left her, she formed her own record label, Bonanza Records, in July of 1968. Then, at the suggestion of Durwood Haddock, who had a little publishing and booking business in the same building where Mother had her offices, she decided to get an all-girl band together and book some appearances or tours. Mother started recruiting female musicians from all over. Dee Bolling, who replaced Erma Williams as Mother's secretary, has described what that endeavor was like.

> It's really difficult keeping an all-girl band together, no matter who you are. You get promotional pictures made, and by the time you get to the date, maybe you still have one or two of the same ones in the group. The band was good. Audrey would work them and work them. The problem was that she was drinking while she was working. I think she would get upset about going on the stage, and then she just couldn't go on straight. I'm sure she had to live up to this image that she had helped to create, and she just couldn't handle it without a pill or a drink.

The first show for the all-girl band Audrey Williams and the Cold, Cold Hearts was in Huntsville, Alabama. I went to see the show. I could hardly wait. I had never heard Audrey sing, and I was horrified. I wanted to go up and say, "Audrey, let's go home." I really did. I could tell she had been drinking, and I couldn't handle it. She knew, too. She didn't play games with people that knew her.

The one thing I think Audrey failed to understand was that she didn't have to sing. She didn't have to do anything. People would book her in their clubs just because she was Mrs. Hank Williams. Had she ever really understood the impact she had on people, things would have gone a lot differently. She understood the impact the name Hank Williams had, but for some reason she didn't get the idea that she could just show up and give an interview or anything and people would turn out for it. Country Music fans are very loyal.

The all-girl band was Mother's last all-out effort to create something that was completely her own, and she pushed it in her typical style, with no holds barred. Buddy Lee recalls some of Mother's tactics in promoting the band.

Audrey called me one day in 1969. She wanted me to come down to the house and see the all-girl band she was putting together. Bud Wendell from the Opry was there, and we all had a few drinks. I didn't know Bud was going to be there, and he didn't know I was going to be there. We listened to the group, and she told me she wanted me to book them and I said all right. She had had a few drinks by this time, and she told Bud Wendell she wanted him to put the girls on the Saturday night Opry. He said he would when he had an open spot. She said, "Dammit, I mean this Saturday night." He said it wasn't the group and it wasn't her. He just already had everyone lined up for that night. She asked me to tell him to put them on, and he had the same answer. So she got mad at both of us. "If you don't like the group, you can both get out right now," she said.

When Audrey didn't drink, she was still sharp, but after two or more drinks, she could be unreasonable. If she asked me to get her a menthol cigarette, I knew I was in trouble because she only smoked when she got to drinking a lot. The next day after a scene like that, she'd call and apologize, though, and a lot of people wouldn't. She'd say, "Aw, Honey, you know I didn't mean that." It was hard to stay mad at her.

When Mother's band did make it onto the "Grand Ole Opry" at a later date, there was a problem with some costumes she had ordered for the girls' Opry debut. After the band finally came out on stage, it took them the longest time to get started. That occasion was a disaster, says Grant Turner, who was emceeing a portion of the show.

One of the people who was closest to Mother in her last years was Tina Smith from Milledgeville, Georgia. In February 1970 she became a drummer in Mother's all-girl band. Tina, Maxie Carter, the piano player, and Sylvia Gares, the steel player, lived at the house with Mother, so they had the chance to see all sides of her. On several occasions, they saw her change from sweet to defiant ("ain't nobody gonna tell me what to do") to hateful in a space of thirty minutes. According to Tina, Mother was lonely even on the road with the band.

> Audrey would keep to herself most of the time. A third of the bus was hers, and that's where she spent most of her time between engagements. When she wasn't drinking, she was sleeping. Every now and then she'd get out, and we'd all go in somewhere to eat, but that didn't happen often. Unless she was on the stage, it was like she didn't want to be seen in the public eye. It was like she had to be almost perfect before she would let anyone see her, and she didn't look very terrific when she was on one of her binges.
>
> We would make an attempt to go into her bedroom and talk to her. She was just so lonely, and I hated to see her live that way.
>
> Audrey missed Hank, Sr., like no one would believe. She had a jukebox that she kept in the music room, and in the summertime she'd put it out by the pool. I remember one night we came in and that jukebox was going so loud that we heard it up on Franklin Road. It was some song by Hank, Sr. I knew from then on whenever that happened she was depressed about Hank, Sr. Those were the only times she would ever talk about him, and then she'd just talk about the good times. It would all start in the bedroom when she'd take out his pictures and old things that belonged to him. I'd say that that happened about once or twice a month while I was there.

Mother closed down her offices in the 812 Building in summer 1970, and not long after that her all-girl band broke up.

Booking the group had become nearly impossible, and Mother was getting to be a very sick woman.

Mother's family in Alabama had not understood how much to blame her drinking was for all that was happening to her, but they began to see through it when she gave her parents a fiftieth wedding anniversary party down there in November 1969. We had a lot of guests, and Mother had spent a lot of money. She got the press to come and write it up, but Hank, Jr., didn't come, and she had really wanted him to be there.

As the day progressed, Mother began to drink some, and by the time all the guests had left except her sisters and their kids, Mother was about drunk. When she was drunk, her self-control would break down and she'd start crying. She started talking about Hank, Jr., why he didn't come, and how it would have meant a lot to her and Grandmama and Granddaddy.

She'd cry, and then somebody would say something she didn't particularly like. She'd flare off, just kind of raise her voice and tell them they were wrong. Mother was very hard to deal with because you can't reason with somebody who's drunk. She'd go from room to room and cry some more and talk some more, and she ended up ruining the day for everybody. The next day she felt bad about it and called everybody to tell them she was sorry.

But when you're an alcoholic, you're an alcoholic, and once you start to drink, you just don't have any control over what you're doing. She never would admit she was an alcoholic, though. She never did want to admit that she was that weak.

When the time came for our third child, Michelle, to be born on July 30, 1970, Lamar was on tour with Hank, Jr., and Mother was out of town. My best friend Delila Keith (now Ellis) took me to the hospital and stayed with me until Michelle was born. When I went home, she came and took care of us until Lamar could get back home.

As sick as she was, Mother came to stay with us for two weeks, too. During that time she cleaned, cooked, and took care of everybody. At that time, Ricky, our oldest child, was nine, and Tawana was four and a half years old.

Mother didn't like for Lamar to go out on the road if I had a new baby or was sick, even when she was booking Hank, Jr.'s act. Mother worried about people a lot more than everybody realized she did. She wanted her family to have everything, and that included her sisters, mother, and daddy — anybody who was close kin to her. She took care of her family all of her life.

That fall Mother was close to dying. She couldn't keep anything down and had diarrhea, but the doctors couldn't determine what was wrong with her. After tests and x-rays, a specialist was called in, and he figured out that Mother's first surgery was the problem. The operation had been done correctly at the time, but since then they had learned that rerouting the intestines of a thin person could cause a blockage later on. They had to remove quite a bit of her intestines in her second operation because there was so much poison in her system.

In mid-November *Billboard* stated that "Audrey Williams underwent surgery last week and is on the mend." Also, "her son, Hank, Jr., showed up for a visit just prior to the operation. The reconciliation came at a great time." Mother was back at home before Christmas.

Miss Ragland had left Mother in 1969 when the members of the all-girl band were first living at the house and about to go out on the road. "I was always having to take the girls someplace. And anyway, Mrs. Williams made me mad, so I left then and there," says Miss Ragland. But when Mother was in the hospital the second time, she went back to the house to check on some things for Mother and stayed on to take care of her after she came home.

"I always thought I would leave when the children got older," Miss Ragland explained, "but it didn't work out that way. As soon as they got older, I could see that she needed me worse than they did. She would say, 'Now, you won't leave me this time if I get rough, will you?' Sometimes she'd say the ugliest things to me when she was drinking, but when she wasn't drinking, she was as sweet as could be. No matter what, though, Mrs. Williams never treated me as a servant. She treated me like a member of the family. She'd always apologize to me when she'd straighten out, too. She'd say, 'I'm sorry that I treated you like I did. I used to be treated that way, too.'"

Even though Mother's sickness from drinking and pills did not pull her down as fast as Daddy's did, it did the very same thing to her — it changed her basic personality from good to bad. Everybody who knew Mother gives the same story. When she was drinking, she was a completely different person.

I had to admit that I didn't want to be around her when she was drinking. Mother would talk ugly and get mad at me because I was trying to say, "Mother, don't drink so much" every way I knew how. She would say, "You don't care nothing about me anyway, and if that's all you have to say to me, just get out and leave me alone. I don't want you here."

She never apologized to me, though, and I'd just try to ignore it. She used to say she didn't remember anything she did when she got drunk. Maybe she didn't. I don't think she wanted to remember. I wish I could have helped her some way. Her and Daddy, too.

The first time Mother tried to kill herself, she took sleeping pills and had to have her stomach pumped at Miller's clinic. I raced out there when they called me and asked Dr. Miller, who had been our family doctor for many years, if there was anything I could do. He told me, "Lycrecia, your mother is a self-destructive person. She feels like she needs to be punished. She doesn't want to hurt anybody else but herself, but people like that always do hurt those around them. One day she will destroy herself, and the bad part is, you'll have to watch and won't be able to do anything about it." He was right.

Mother was arrested twice during the summer of 1972. In De Funiak Springs, Florida, she was charged with drunken driving, resisting arrest, and destroying county property. She refused to get out of her car when she was stopped and then broke about a dozen windows in the county jail while waiting for the bondsman to post her $750 bond. Then, in Brantley, Alabama, she was arrested for "driving while intoxicated." She was held at the St. Charles Motel in Luverne until some Alabama State troopers delivered her safely to the home of her close friend, Ruby Folsom Austin, in Montgomery.

Mother and Daddy had known Ruby back in their Montgomery days, when her brother, Big Jim Folsom, was the governor of Alabama and Ruby was his acting first lady. She and Mother would fuss and fight sometimes, but they remained as close as sisters for over twenty years. Ruby was a heavy drinker, too, and with her, Mother could drink to her heart's content, talk, and party with her friends, and not have to explain anything to anybody.

Mother's problems with the law went beyond being stopped and arrested for drunken driving. In about 1969, she approached attorney James Neal about helping her straighten out her terrible financial situation. She owed a tremendous amount of money to the IRS. She had stopped drinking for several weeks, and she knew she needed his help.

Jim Neal had met Mother back in 1966 when Marathon Pictures was being dissolved. He remembers her as a difficult client, but a lovely, kind, and extremely generous person. He felt very sorry for Mother because he learned that many people took advantage of her generosity. His goal was to get Mother's finances back in order, to reduce her debts and arrange to pay off the IRS. With Mother's permission, he took complete control over her money. He signed the checks, paid the bills, and put her on a limited expense account.

For a while, she did exactly as he said, and everything was going fine. He was even getting her out of debt with the IRS. Then I guess she'd begun to drink again, and she wouldn't listen to him anymore. "If you're not going to listen to me," he told her, "you might as well take all of it back and just do whatever you want to."

Mother said, "O.K., I'll have Lycrecia sign the checks, and that way I won't spend so much money." So she took me up to meet with James, and he proceeded to tell me what he had done, how much Mother still owed the IRS, and what she needed to do to pay it off.

At the time, I think she owed the IRS around ninety thousand dollars. She had just gotten a royalty check for about that amount, and he told me she should pay the IRS half of it and then try to budget the rest for living expenses.

I sat there until he finished telling me all this, and then I asked, right in front of Mother, "James, do you think for one minute that she's going to listen to me when I say, 'Mother, I'm not going to sign this check for you?'" He said, "No, but that is what she thinks she wants at the moment." He told me he'd help me carry all of her stuff out because it wasn't his responsibility anymore. As we walked out, I knew I was going to have to put up with a lot.

After she left James Neal, her finances got progressively worse. She never bothered to pay the IRS any more, so they just started adding on penalties until she owed them so much they threatened to seize her property.

The last couple of years of Mother's life I tried everything I knew to help her. I went to attorneys and I went to psychiatrists; but nothing panned out.

I can tell you from personal experience that it is not easy to do anything for alcoholics. Unless they do something voluntarily, you have to take legal steps to declare that they are completely incompetent mentally and have them committed to a sanitarium. I was not going to do that to Mother; she had had enough embarrassment in her life. It might have saved her life — I don't know — but I just could not bring myself to do it.

I kept trying to get her to go into the hospital and get herself straightened out, but she wouldn't. When she'd get in real bad shape, though, she'd call me and want me to do something to help her. One time I arranged for her to go to a hospital in Memphis. Hank, Jr., said he'd pay for it, but they could only keep her as long as she was willing to stay. I told the doctor that as soon as she was sober and got a little strength back, she would walk out. She did.

After that experience, I went to see a psychiatrist named Dr. Nat Winston. We talked for a long time. Dr. Winston suggested I just go down to the police station and tell them I wanted to have my mother picked up and taken to Parkview Hospital. We'd get her in that way. I thought, "Oh good! At least here's a way!" I called my friend Carla Norrell and asked her to come with me because I didn't know how well I could handle things on my own.

I went up to see the judge and told him I wanted him to send someone out to pick up my mother and have her committed to the hospital for alcohol and drug abuse. He asked me if I had two doctors to commit her, and I said, "No, sir. Dr. Winston told me that you could arrange to have her picked up, and he would notify the hospital." The judge told me they couldn't carry her out to the hospital unless a doctor had called and said she was going to be committed. All they could do was hold her in the jail until Dr. Winston could get there. When I heard that, I just hit the floor. I called Dr. Winston and he said, "Lord, no, don't do that to her. She couldn't take that." He wanted to think about it and see what else he could come up with, but I was so depressed, I was ready to give up.

This was about the same period when Mother tried to kill herself for the second time. Flossie had been out to the house to cook and Mother wanted her to stay over, but Flossie couldn't. Mother said, "Well, go on, go on and leave me." She seemed pretty straight, but when Flossie went to get her coat, Mother buzzed her and said, "Flossie, come in here, I've cut my wrists."

Flossie called me from the hospital to ask if I could come up and see about Mother because they wanted to keep her over. I ran up there, but she had already called a taxi and left. I thought, *You're worrying everybody to death. Why can't you admit you have a problem?*

When I got to the house, boy was I mad! The cab was there, but Mother didn't have her keys and the house was locked up. I had to call Mother's yard man, L. N., and ask him to come back over and let us in.

I got her into the bed. Her wrists were all bandaged, and she needed help. I asked her why she did this and she said, "I don't know, Honey. I thought I wanted to die, but when I saw all the blood it scared me, so I called Flossie." I told her to get some rest and went into the den to watch TV. I heard her get up. She said she wanted a drink.

"No, ma'am, I'm not going to get you anything to drink," I said.

"I just want to settle my nerves," she told me. "I need one drink to relax me."

I told her I wouldn't get it for her, and she said, "O.K., I'll just get it myself then."

"Mother, please don't drink," I begged her.

"Honey," she said, "I'm just going to have this one drink, and then I'm going to bed."

I had had it. I said, "Mother, if you have a drink, I'm leaving. I have a family, and I left them to come take care of you. If you don't care enough about yourself to stay sober, I'm leaving." She just went back to bed.

Now I realize that she just needed the attention. She hadn't actually cut her wrists bad enough to kill herself, just like she hadn't taken enough pills the other time to really do herself in. She was just scared and lonely.

About the middle of 1973, Mother started one last big undertaking. She decided to finish the wing on the house and open a museum for the country music tourists who were flocking to Nashville. She talked Dee Bolling into coming back to work for her, and they worked hard when Mother was able. This would have helped her finances except that she went overboard on getting the best for the house. She ordered gold fixtures in the bathroom and Italian marble for floors. She was having a large portrait of Daddy painted and getting a film about him ready to be shown on the tours.

Up to a point, everything looked like it was going to work out. Then the city of Oak Hill filed suit to prevent her from running the museum.

The city said that if they let Mother do it, they'd have to let everybody else do it and it would cause traffic jams and complaints from the neighbors. On Franklin Road where we lived, it wouldn't have been a problem, but in the smaller neighborhoods where the houses were closer together it would. The city won their case on grounds that the zoning didn't allow commercialism.

Mother pressed on though, planning the "biggest and best garage sale in Nashville's history" for Friday and Saturday, November 8–9, 1974. The idea was to clear out some of her furniture, antiques, jewelry, and clothing and also to sell Hank Williams photographs, T-shirts, and souvenirs to promote the new museum. She never intended to sell any of Daddy's personal belongings, but the *Nashville Banner*'s headline on November fifth, "Cleaning Out Hank Williams' Attic," plus other similar publicity gave many people the wrong idea.

There were other reasons, too, why the sale didn't turn out to be the kind of thing that Mother originally had in mind. For one thing, some of her Gatlinburg friends who were antique dealers had asked if they could set up there, but then took advantage of the situation by offering estate jewelry at outrageous prices. This caused a lot of bad publicity, as did the two-dollar admission charge to go into the house to keep out curiosity seekers. The main reason that things got out of hand, however, was Mother herself.

When I got to the house that first day, I tried to get her not to even come out. She was already drunk by mid-day. I didn't want her to do any interviews because I knew that the reporters would have a field day, and they did.

I didn't even come for the second day. Mother had always had so much pride in herself when I was growing up, and I really looked up to her when she was younger. She always wanted to make a good impression on people, but then to see what alcohol and pills had done to her — I couldn't stand to be around her when she got like that. She knew what was happening to her, but she couldn't do anything about it. I was embarrassed for her.

Mother had been trying to get Daddy's belongings back home for a long time. In an interview several months after she finally got everything back, Mother described her reaction when it all arrived: "I do now have all of [Hank's] clothes and things. . . . They'd been in Montgomery, Alabama in storage. But you'll never know the feeling I had when these clothes came in. I knew the driver of the truck [and] he was practically shaking when he came to the door. He couldn't hardly wait to get these things to their destination because he realized that he was hauling valuable merchandise . . . Memories . . . that night . . . I talked to him a lot that night, I said, 'Well, Hank, after twenty years I finally got your things home.'"

Dee Bolling describes what happened when Daddy's things were brought into the house:

> We weren't expecting anything to arrive that day, and the people just pulled up in a big truck and started bringing these big boxes in. Audrey had them put it all in this room in the new part of the house down the corridor from the office. After it was all in there, she closed the door to the room and came back up and told me, "Dolores, Honey, you just close up early and go on home." That's all she said to me, and she just whipped down the hall, moving very quickly. I heard her pull the double doors to and lock them.
>
> She couldn't wait to get out of there. The energy was so suffocating that you just couldn't hardly get a breath. It was a huge

area, but it felt like there was no air left in it. I was really concerned about Audrey because I could tell she really could not
handle it. Besides, I could not understand — it was such a big area
and these were just a few little things that they moved into one
room and it seemed like it consumed that whole end of the house.
I was not afraid that Audrey would do anything to herself, but I
was just really worried about her well-being. I was thinking I had
to get out of there, too, but I also was thinking, "How can she
stay?" There was no reason for me to feel anything, either, because
I was not emotionally attached to Hank Williams. I actually knew
very little about him.

The next day when I came in, she had bounced right back and
everything was calm. Audrey could make remarkable recoveries.
You would leave her in the afternoon and you'd think, "My good-
ness, this is going to take her a long time to get over," and you'd
see her the next morning and it was just like the day before had
never happened. I don't think we did anything much for a couple
of days, and then she went into the room on her own and started
looking through everything and unpacking.

Things were never the same after that day. Before then, when I
first had my office out there, there were so many things that
weren't finished. There was just a big, empty feeling about it, but
no particular personality. But after that day there was a totally
different feeling there. Everything was different — it smelled different, it felt different, there were different sights and sounds.

At that point Mother opened the museum to the public in
spite of the Oak Hill ruling. She bought a mini-bus and hired a
driver, John Wilson, and created her own little tour company.
The tourists got to see a short film and then to go into the room
filled with large glass cases displaying Daddy's belongings.

John Wilson's young friend, Johnny Barnes, a management
trainee at the Third National Bank at the time, would come
over to the house on weekends to run the movie projector for
the museum tours. He and John Wilson had helped Mother
unpack the boxes of Daddy's clothing, instruments, and other
personal effects. Johnny remembers that there were bundles of
shirts, at least one hundred ties, cowboy suits, hats and boots,
guitars, a fiddle, a tape recorder, and Daddy's baggage, including a little overnight bag with a hairbrush, toothbrush and Pep-
sodent toothpaste in it. They hung everything up and arranged

it in the glass cases, matching items of clothing with pictures of Hank wearing those same articles. "It was quite an experience for me," says Johnny, "it was like history unfolding."

Audrey was a real strong person, despite her health. And strong people, you either like them or you hate them. She never used it against me, but others who might think they were big-time and question her abilities, she'd still stand right up to them. I could see it, especially when she was drinking, a sense of power, an implied "Don't you dare mess with me, I'm Audrey Williams, Mrs. Hank Williams." So if that's the only time you ever saw her, you would think negative of her. I could see, too, all I had read and heard about her — the drive, the ambition, the desire to be the best. But she had certain morals about getting there. She was just a real sweet lady.

We didn't discuss Hank, Sr., a lot, but everything she said, it was him that caused the problems with his drinking and stuff. I could see where she'd just had enough of him and him drinking and carousing and had finally put her foot down. But she wasn't bitter. She had a lot of feelings for him still. I remember in her bedroom she had a little framed Mother's Day card from him that read, "Audrey, I love you." She didn't save anything gaudy, just some real nice, personal mementos.

Audrey was open and kind-hearted to people, but a lot of those who came over would take advantage of her. I've seen people there partying and hoping that she would be passed out so they could have free access to the house. I didn't like to be there when any of those other characters were there because I didn't want to be responsible for them or to be associated with what was going on when they were there.

There was a period where she was getting some threats and she was of a mind that it really scared her to be in that house alone at night. She had asked me and John Wilson if we'd take turns for awhile just staying there with her. We were both single, so we didn't have to be anywhere and we were glad to help her. When I got there one evening after work, there was a couple over there, a young girl and an older guy. I asked them where was Audrey, and the girl said she gave her some pills and she was out. So I went and looked and she was in bed, and they were drunk and just roaming the house. Finally they left. I stayed there all night on the sofa in the den, and Audrey was just out the whole time. She kept the museum locked, but all anyone had to do was go get the keys, and Lord knows if anything was ever stolen. Once someone stole a remote control from the television just because it came from the house. She didn't have that many parties, but when she did people would be just roaming at will. Early on she'd be out of it, but people would be there all night. She'd just have her fill and retire back there and take her pills or whatever, and no one would bother her.

We'd take Audrey out some, John and I. Once she came to a softball game I was playing. On another occasion we had a picnic out in the country, and she liked that. Several times we'd go to this pizza place and just talk. She wouldn't drink. We'd just eat pizza. And sometimes we just drove around town and we'd ask her questions, and she'd tell us stories and we'd all laugh. One night she had me and John over for supper and she cooked this jambalaya-type dish. She went to a lot of trouble to make a nice meal for us, and we sat out back and ate and had a great evening. She just got worse and worse, though. The more she drank and the more I'd go over and she'd be drunk, the less I wanted to go over. I was afraid I'd walk in one time and find her dead.

Mother's relationship with Hank, Jr., had been off and on ever since their split in 1968. She attended his second wedding, in April 1971 to Gwen Yeargain. In September 1972 *Billboard* reported that "Hank Williams, Jr., who will become a father in December, has ended his estrangement with his mother, Audrey Williams, and now spends considerable time with her, which has improved her health, her disposition, and everything else."

But that was not quite the whole story. Hank, Jr., was going through his own personal hell throughout that period, with his failing second marriage, a suicide attempt, and leaving his long-term manager Buddy Lee. Hank, Jr., was also starting his own battle with too much money, alcohol, and drugs. "The only person I felt close to," he later wrote, "was Daddy, and he was dead. I understood him . . . like I never understood him before." In 1974 Hank, Jr., moved down to Cullman, Alabama, and Mother was, of course, unhappy over the move.

In early 1975 we knew the IRS was about to take both the little house next door on Franklin Road and the chalet in Gatlinburg. Mother kept saying she'd take care of clearing out the chalet; she had some very nice things there. I'd wait a while and then ask, "Mother, did you ever go get the furniture from the chalet?" and she'd say, "Well, no . . ." Erma Williams says taking the furniture out would have been admitting that it could happen, so Mother refused. She reasoned that if she left the furniture, they couldn't take the house. Erma was with Mother when she finally did go.

"She wanted to go to Gatlinburg, and when we got there, there was already a sign on the door and it was padlocked. She broke the heel off her shoe trying to open it and then went to the car and got the jack and a screwdriver, anything she could find to get that lock off of the door. She was ready to break the glass on the sliding glass door, but I warned her, 'Don't do this Audrey. You're breaking and entering now.' 'Not my own chalet,' she argued. It was nighttime and I did talk her into leaving it alone, telling her we'd come back in the morning."

Finally I decided I would just do it myself, but by then it was too late. An attorney wrote the IRS a letter to help me get back everything that was inside the house, but we never got any response. I think the chalet went for twelve thousand dollars, and the house next door sold for a very low price.

Then, after the chalet and the other house were gone, her attorneys told her that if she'd just give me the power of attorney to take care of her business, that the IRS couldn't do anything more to her for awhile. When she was lucid, when she wasn't so full of pills and stuff, she'd say, "O.K., draw up the papers, and I'll sign them." Then the day would come, and I'd go trooping up there and find her drinking or high on pills, and she wouldn't sign the paper. That happened two or three times. She was not going to give me power of attorney.

Later, I'd call and say, "Mother, you know I'd never do anything that was not in your best interests. I'll talk things over with you, and you'll be included in everything we do. This is just to prevent the IRS from taking your house." She'd say, "I know it, Honey, I'll call and tell them to drop the papers off, and we'll get it done," but she never did. She just would not let go of being in control, even if it meant her destruction.

About this same time, in mid-March of 1975, a jury in Nashville was listening to arguments presented by attorneys for Daddy's second wife, Billie Jean Berlin. Although she had remarried twice since Daddy's death, she was pressing her case to certain inheritances as his widow.

Litigation with Billie Jean had a nearly seven-year history, dating back to November 1968, when she filed suit in the federal courts of Atlanta, Georgia, against MGM Pictures. She claimed that the film *Your Cheatin' Heart* damaged her reputation because it portrayed Daddy still being married to his first wife at the time of his death.

In the 1975 case the legality of Billie Jean's marriage to Daddy was again the key issue, but this time she was pressing for nothing less than the ownership to Mother's half of the second twenty-eight years of copyrights to Daddy's songs. On October 22, 1975, the marriage was declared both "putative" in Louisiana and "common-law" in Alabama. U.S. Judge L. Clure Morton also ruled that day that Billie Jean had not signed away her widow's rights to the copyright renewals when she accepted the pay off after Daddy's death.

The royalties were still coming to Mother during this time, but the decision was a blow. The incredible debts that she was accumulating on the house took so much money that she sometimes didn't have any left to buy groceries or pay her help. Erma came back for the last months, and between us we made some progress in paying off the contractors, but we weren't able to pay the IRS.

Then Hank, Jr., got hurt. On August 8, 1975, he was hiking on Ajax Mountain along the edge of the Continental Divide with his friend Dick Willey and Dick's eleven-year-old son, Walt. Hank, Jr., lost his footing and fell head-first down the mountainside. His friends watched in horror as he somersaulted hundreds of feet down the mountainside until a huge pile of rocks stopped him head-on. His body was bruised, but his face and head had taken most of the blows. Most of his face was gone, his head was split open, and his brain was exposed. Dick and his son climbed down to Hank. He was just sitting there, and when he touched his face, he said, "Oh, my God, my face is gone!" Dick told him no, it wasn't gone. Dick tied his shirt around Hank's face and head as well as he could, and then they helped Hank over to a tree and set him down. Dick then left his terrified son with instructions to do whatever he had to do to keep Hank awake, and raced off to find help. It was nearly eight hours after the accident before the helicopter delivered Hank, Jr., to the Community Hospital in Missoula, Montana. All through this ordeal, Hank never lost consciousness. At the hospital, three surgeons spent seven and a half hours putting him back together again.

Mother flew to Montana immediately. When I got out there the next day, Mother told me, "Honey, don't let it scare you when you see Hank, Jr. He is really really messed up." I thought he would be all cut up. His head was all bandaged up and very swollen, but the rest looked all right. As critical as he was, Hank wrote me a note saying, "I know someone that has a birthday in a few days." It was my birthday on August 13, four days later.

Later we were eating at the hotel, and Mother said, "Honey, I've got to go to the bathroom." When she came back, I could tell that she'd had a drink. There was that much of a difference in her.

"Mother," I begged, "please don't drink. You really need to stay straight."

"Don't worry about me, Honey," she said. "I'm not going to drink. Everything's going to be all right."

I was staying in the room with Mother that night, and she took a handful of tranquilizers. "I'm so upset over Hank, Jr., Honey," she explained, "that I have to have that many to sleep." I thought maybe if I didn't preach at her she'd be O.K.

She was all right the next day, but that night she was drinking again and we got into an argument. Finally I said, "Mother, I've got to go back home. Why don't you fly back with me, and then you can come back later?"

"Oh no, Honey," she told me, "I can't leave Hank, Jr."

"Well," I suggested, "if you're going to stay, why don't you try to stay straight so you can help him."

"I will, Honey," she promised. "I will."

I left, but she stayed till just before they let Hank, Jr., out of the hospital, and I'm sure she didn't keep her word about not drinking. And when she got home, she just went to bed and would cry and say over and over, "My beautiful, beautiful son . . ."

From the time of Hank, Jr.'s accident on, Mother was more or less of an invalid, almost never leaving her bedroom. She had lost a lot of weight because she couldn't or wouldn't eat, and Erma would have to call a visiting nurse to give her some glucose intravenously. Mother began to have seizures (the doctor had told her she had become epileptic and she was under medication for it).

Erma can recall only one time that Mother got out of bed, dressed, and went out of the house during those last months. She wanted to go down to Rossville, Georgia, right outside of Chattanooga, to see a well-known spiritualist named Doc Anderson who lived there. She had been to see him once or twice before and had talked to him often on the telephone, but she felt the need to see him in person again and ask him about Hank, Jr.

"I didn't believe in that stuff," says Erma, "but I took her anyway. When she came out, she said, 'Erma, it's the strangest thing. He sat there and just looked at me and would not talk about anything. He wouldn't even take my money. Can you believe that? I kept asking him questions about my son, what's going to happen to my beautiful son, but he wouldn't tell me anything.' I get chill bumps just thinking about it now, because I remember as we were driving home I had this strange feeling like, 'Does Audrey have a future?' I remember driving and thinking, 'What happens if she doesn't have a future? What can you do if someone is going to die?'"

I guess Mother couldn't see any reason to live, much less stay straight.

The little house and chalet were gone, the city of Oak Hill had finally closed down the museum, Hank, Jr. had gone back to Alabama, and now he was seriously injured, maybe handicapped forever, and Billie Jean was trying to get the copyrights to Daddy's catalog. But that was not the end of the crises that Mother was facing.

Her mother and my grandmama, Artie Mae Sheppard, had had to have more cobalt treatments for a recurrence of cancer and was recuperating at home in Banks. Mother had talked to Grandmama nearly every day of her life, so the prospect of her death was devastating. According to Erma, though, if ever there was a time that Mother really got close to her daddy, it was during those months, because they suffered together.

The final blow for Mother, and the one which she absolutely

refused to take, was the idea of the IRS taking her home. "They'll never take me out of this house alive," she told me.

Mother had always promised to leave the house to me as compensation for not allowing Daddy to adopt me and entitle me to a share of his estate. Whenever the time would come to formalize this in her will, though, she couldn't do it. She was afraid doing that would hurt Hank, Jr. She did feel guilty that Hank, Jr., had so much from Daddy's royalties and I had gotten nothing and was unprotected if something should happen to Lamar, but she could not bring herself to sign a will that would cut Hank, Jr., out.

I was in and out of the house as much as I could be with small children at home, but Erma was with Mother a good bit those last weeks.

"Audrey would be in bed," says Erma, "and we would just sit and talk and talk for eight or ten hours sometimes.

"Women do not usually sit around and talk about the intimate parts of their relationships, but during one of those talking sessions shortly before she died, Audrey told me something about that part of her life with Hank. 'I have to tell you about this dream I had,' she said. Now Audrey did not dream that much because her sleep was usually so drugged, but this time she did. She had a dream that Hank Williams had come back, had come into her room, and they had made love. She said, 'Erma, it was so unbelievable because I woke up and I felt in the bed for him, the dream was so real.' She had felt such a love, such a warmth that it seemed totally real to her. She said that he had told her he loved her and everything was going to be all right."

"It was during these times that I really learned about prayer," says Erma, "and it never has left my mind. Audrey said, 'Erma, God will get me out of this. God, please, you've got to get me out of this!' Audrey's relationship with God was that she would tell Him what to do just like she did other people. I'm sure God understood her, though, because she had asked Him to get her out of her problems and He did — the day before the IRS was going to come and take her home."

Chapter 16

Mother's Gone, Too

A couple of weeks before Mother died, her old friend Doris Davis came out to the house to visit. Doris's recollection of the day clearly shows the state of mind Mother was in as she neared the end.

Audrey was in her bathroom off the bedroom when I came in. When she came out, she was just kind of holding on to the furniture to get back to bed, she was so weak. She said, "Don't I look awful?" and I said, "Well, if you had your makeup on and your hair fixed, you'd look like you always did." I sat down on a hassock she had by the bed, and we just reminisced about old times. She wanted me to move out there with her, but I told her I couldn't do that. I had a house of my own.

I said I was going back to get a beer. I had brought a six-pack for myself and put them in the refrigerator, and she said she'd like one, too. So I got her a beer and poured her about half a glass of it. When I came back from getting the beer, she had a handful of pills she was swallowing, and she dropped some on the floor. I said, "Audrey, are you taking all those pills?" and she said it was O.K. The doctor had given them to her. She said sometimes she had to take as many as twelve pills at night to get to sleep, and I told her that was too many. But she said that she was strong and could handle it.

We were just sitting there talking, she was sitting on the edge of the bed, and all of a sudden she looked at me and said, "Who are you, and what are you doing in my house?"

I was taken aback, but I just said, "Audrey, I'm Doris."

"That doesn't mean anything to me," she told me. "Did you

come out here to spy on me or Hank, Jr.? I've never seen you before. What are you doing in my house?"

It was frightening to me. We were there all alone, so I tried another tactic. I said, "Audrey, come off that shit. You know damn well who I am. I'm Doris!"

"Well, that shocked her back into reality and she said, "Oh Doris, I'm sorry!" and she broke down and fell on the bed crying. Her mind would just come and go like that. It was pitiful. I hated to see her like that because she was always so vivacious before she got sick.

Then she wanted to get out of bed and down on her knees, and she wanted me to come over by her and pray. She wanted to pray for Hank, Jr. I had to get her back in bed, and then she'd want to pray again. I thought, *If she prays one more time, I don't think I can get her back in that bed.*

She cried and begged me not to go, and I hated to leave her there by herself, but I couldn't stay. I told her, "Honey, I'm going to have to go, but you stay in bed and rest." I got her back in bed after praying three or four times and covered her up and thought if something happens to her and they find her dead, I'd feel horrible about it. I couldn't stand to see her like that, but there wasn't anything more I could do to help her.

There didn't seem to be anything anybody could do to help Mother. She had lost Hank, Jr., she had lost her health, she had lost the copyrights to Billie Jean, she had lost the museum, her mother was dying, she had only the house left, and she was about to lose that. Mother was a fighter, but she was so tired. She was ready to give up the fight. The last straw emotionally was the house.

It was during this time that Bernice Turner was in Nashville on her way to take her son Robbie to play steel guitar with a group in Georgia. When she saw how badly Mother was doing, she sent Robbie on down to Georgia and stayed to help her. After a few days, Mother seemed to be getting better, and Bernice decided to run a couple of errands.

Before I left, though, I had looked everywhere and made sure there was not anything around for her to drink. I couldn't have been gone for more than three hours, and when I got back, I found her on the floor where she had been crawling back to the bed from the bathroom with a bottle of vodka. When I touched her, she was cold as ice and it scared me to death. But I saw that she wasn't dead, so I picked her up and carried her back to bed.

The following day my son's amplifier broke down in Georgia, and I had to go take him another one. I hated to leave Audrey, though, so I talked to Erma and said, "Please don't leave her by herself." When Audrey found out I was going to leave, she said that was all right. She just wanted to be left alone, anyhow. I told her she didn't need to be alone just then.

I was very upset about leaving. I told her I was just going to take the new amplifier down to Robbie and come back to Memphis to get some clothes, and then I'd be back. She had evidently got back to drinking that morning while I was busy getting things in the car. I had found what she had left in the bathroom the day before, but obviously she had some somewhere else. She had come in and sat on the couch when I was leaving, and I started crying. I went over to her, and I hugged her and said, "Please Audrey. Please don't die like Hank did," and she said, "Well, if I do, then I'll be with him." I left crying.

Shortly after Bernice left, Tina [Smith] called Mother and said that she and a friend were coming to Nashville and wanted to see her. Erma tried to explain that Mother was just too sick for company, but Tina was insistent. She just knew the Lord had put Audrey on her heart for a reason, and she wanted to pray with her. According to Erma, Mother was glad to see Tina because she was into praying at the time.

The day after Bernice left, Audrey's accountant had called and told me he'd done all he could, but the IRS was coming on November 5, the next Wednesday, to seize the house. When he called, he first asked to talk to Audrey and I told him she was on the phone with her mother, and was there anything I could do. That's when he told me the IRS was going to seize the house. Just about the time he said that, Audrey picked up the phone, which she normally did not do, and heard "IRS seize the house." So she cut in and she said, "Jerry, that's all right with me. They can come and see the house. I don't mind." Jerry said, "No . . . ," and I tried to stop him, I said, "Jerry, we'll talk about this later," but he didn't catch my meaning and finished telling her that they were going to take the house.

"What!" Audrey screamed. "They're not taking my house! I'll shoot anybody that tries to come in and take this house!" We tried to talk to her, Jerry and I, but she was adamant. "I'll kill them!" she swore. "They'll never get in here!" They wouldn't have, either. I believe she would have shot them and gone to jail because that house was all she had left in the world and she had put too much of herself into it.

After we got off the phone I called Hank, Jr., to tell him because this was partly his house, too, and maybe he'd want to buy it. He told me, "Go get that gun out of Mama's bedroom." I couldn't find it, though. Later we found out it had been stolen. Audrey was very upset and she started drinking really, really heavily. In the meantime, Tina and her friend arrived.

Tina stayed until Monday morning. She was real helpful with Mother, trying to keep her in bed so she could sleep. It was very difficult to get Mother to eat, and Tina remembers her eating only some watermelon, apple juice, and maybe applesauce.

On Sunday night Mother wouldn't go to sleep or eat, although she finally fell asleep about 4:00 A.M. At five Mother wanted to see Tina.

She wasn't making a whole lot of sense at this particular time, but she did know who I was. She finally went to sleep and seemed to be resting comfortably. Ruth and I did put our ears to her chest real close, and we could hear a rattling in her throat. We didn't really know what it was, but being that she was so sick it could have been anything.

We left the next morning, before lunch. Erma had come in, and we told her what had been going on all weekend. And then we talked to Lycrecia on the phone, and she said that she would be up shortly.

When I found out that the IRS was coming to take the house on Wednesday, November 5, I knew I wasn't going to let them get everything that was inside like they did when they took the chalet. On Monday I called my friend Carla to help me get some of Mother's things out. Mother also had some expensive paintings on loan from an art dealer and some furniture not paid for yet. We called the art dealer and the furniture company to come and get their things.

Erma was already at Mother's house when I arrived, and I

asked her to check on her to see if she was all right. I was afraid I'd wake her up and she would pitch a fit when she found out what I was doing. I asked Erma to go in and check on Mother a couple of more times during the day, because I thought if she saw Erma she wouldn't think anything in particular was going on.

That night Erma and her husband drove by the house on their way home from square dance lessons. They noticed that the outside lights were not on. "Audrey always turned those lights on," Erma says, "always — no matter how sick she was — she got out of the bed and turned those outside lights on. I thought to myself, *Gosh, I wish I'd turned them on because she'll be horrified if she wakes up in the morning and realizes she slept with them off.* She was frightened there all by herself."

The next morning, Tuesday, Flossie called me from the house and said that she had come to do some cooking, but she was worried because Mother hadn't gotten up yet. She asked me if I wanted her to go in and check on her, but I told her not to because I was coming over soon. Flossie had a bad heart, and I was afraid of what she might find if she went in. She told me that Erma was on her way over, so I told her to have Erma check on Mother when she got there and call me.

When I got off the phone with Flossie, I walked into the room where Lamar was sitting, and I said to him, "Honey, my Mother's dead." He tried to tell me that maybe it wasn't so, but I knew inside of me that it was true.

It wasn't long till Erma called and told me she thought Mother was dead. I told her to call an ambulance, and I'd be right there. By the time I got there, the circular drive in front of the house was so filled with vehicles that I had to pull into the driveway next door. Hank, Jr., was already there by then. The date was November 4, 1975.

The autopsy did not find any drugs or alcohol in her body. Mother had run out of her epilepsy medicine the week before, and she had not had the prescription refilled. I feel she knew that not taking the pills would bring on a seizure and she would die and not have to face losing her home.

I decided I would hold Mother's funeral in Montgomery. On November 7 a brief service was held in Troy, Alabama, at the

McGee-Dilliard Funeral Home for Grandmama's benefit because she was too ill to travel to Montgomery. It was Hank,
Jr.'s first public appearance since his accident three months
earlier.

Later that day, Mother's silver and chrome casket was taken
to Montgomery, where Reverend Bob Harrington, the
"Chaplain of Bourbon Street," officiated at her funeral services
at White's Chapel.

After delivering the eulogy, Reverend Harrington turned to
face the casket and spoke these words to Mother: "Hey, good-
lookin', what cha got cookin'? There will be no more cold, cold
heart, no more parting, no more heartache, no more lonely
nights. Audrey will never be lonely again."

At the close of the service, he recited "Beyond The Sunset,"
which Mother had requested to have read at her funeral.

❊   ❊   ❊   ❊   ❊

> Beyond the sunset, O glad reunion,
> With our dear loved ones who've gone before.
> In that fair homeland we'll know no parting,
> Beyond the sunset forever more.

❊   ❊   ❊   ❊   ❊

At the cemetery, Reverend Harrington, referring to Daddy's
nearby grave, commented that, "Just a few feet away rests
enough words for me to use in preaching for the rest of my life.
But now Hank and Audrey have played their last gig." We had
to bury Mother some thirty feet to the left of Daddy's gravesite, not next to him as she had requested.

About one week after Mother's death, I packed up the Franklin
Road house and got her things together. I had taken her picture, the one I always liked so well that she used to keep in her
room, home with me, and it was sitting on my dresser in the
bedroom.

I went in the room one night, and all of a sudden it felt like
she was there in the bedroom with me. I've never had an experience like that before, and it scared me.

I took the picture off my dresser and put it up. I didn't think
she meant to harm me, but it was such a strange feeling. I was

not in a very good state of mind at that time, anyway, I was upset and exhausted. Beside going through Mother's death and the funeral, I was working really hard getting the house emptied out, but as it turned out, the IRS was not able to take the house on Wednesday after all. Because Mother had passed away, it went into her estate.

In November 1977, Mother and Daddy's house and 3.07 acres at 4916 Franklin Road were appraised at approximately $175,000. The condition of the seventeen-room, 10,230-square foot house was considered poor because some areas were still unfinished and the house had not been maintained properly. Because of its piecemeal construction, it was labelled "functionally obsolescent."

The Davidson County Probate Court reported in January 1978 that Mother's estate was $510,636.53 in arrears, including more than $400,000 owed to the IRS. There were insufficient funds to pay the debts. The same report approved the sale of the property for $200,000 dollars, and the IRS settled the case for the selling price of the house. Hank, Jr., and I were advised that if we were to purchase the house, the IRS would not forgive as much of the debt, and estate taxes would have to be paid.

In June 1983, Hank, Jr., and I arranged to have Mother's grave moved next to Daddy's. The twin monuments, enclosed in a small courtyard, overlook the city of Montgomery. Together — in peace — for all time.

✿   ✿   ✿   ✿   ✿

Oh, Heaven only knows how much I miss you,
I can't help it if I'm still in love with you.

To the Reader

Thank you for reading this book. I have been privileged to know Audrey and Hank Williams as Mother and Daddy, and I am happy to be able to share my memories and feelings about them. It has been important to me to share the good times as well as the bad in their lives.

They were genuine people, with real strengths and weaknesses. I can only hope that, after reading about them, you understand why I still love them very, very much.

In 1990 the autobiography *Ain't Nothin' as Sweet as My Baby* by Jett Williams (or Cathy Stone/Dupree, nee Antha Belle Jett) was published, nearly one year after the publication of *Still in Love with You*. Although Jett's book is primarily a personal story of her search for her own identity, it also attempts at times to characterize people and circumstances Jett never knew, such as the marital relationship between Hank and Audrey. Because of that particular misrepresentation and because Lycrecia is asked many questions regarding her feelings about the "Jett Williams issue," this edition of *Still in Love with You* includes her response.

[The Publisher]

A Personal Response to *Ain't Nothin' as Sweet as My Baby*

This is not an easy subject for me to talk about for a number of reasons. In the first place, I know it will be difficult to say what I truly feel and not have it sound like sour grapes or jealousy by those who do not know me. I am going to try, though, because my purpose all along has been to set the record straight and to undo some of the misconceptions people have about Mother, Daddy, Hank, Jr., and me. There are other, more complicated reasons why this is hard to talk about, some that just relate to me personally and some that involve my loyalty to my family. I'll do my best to explain it all as I go along.

Let me make it clear right away that I have nothing against Cathy, or Jett. I sincerely hope her new-found identity will bring her peace of mind and happiness. I have wondered many times, though, why she waited so long to get in touch with me, the only person who really knows what kind of a parent Daddy was. She was in Nashville working with Owen Bradley at the same time I was acting as hostess at our Franklin Road house that had been moved up to Music Row. She could have easily found me then, but she never called until after she had already experienced some legal reversals in her fight to win a part of Daddy's estate. That was not a good time for her to contact me. Hank, Jr., is my brother, and I love him and will always be loyal to him. Cathy is not my blood kin, so she couldn't have expected that I would help her in her battle against Hank, Jr.

Recently, Cathy and I met face to face at the Southern Writers' Festival in Nashville. She had given a short talk about her book, and I was in the audience. She talked about her feelings as an adopted child and that she felt equally close to both of her mothers — the one who raised her and her biological mother, Bobbie, who had died before Cathy could meet her. I had sort of a parallel situation in my life, since I had never seen my own biological father, but I had never cared anything about him. To me, Hank was my daddy and I was satisfied with that. I think Cathy misunderstood my intention in that conversation and thought I was trying to prove that Hank was more *my* father than he was *hers*. Actually, I was just sharing my feelings with her about our similar experiences. After she and I had talked for awhile, my co-author, Dale Vinicur, asked Cathy why she had never gotten in touch with me to find out about Daddy. She said that she *had* called me once and would like very much to talk, but she felt that it was up to me to make the next move. I believe that it's too late now. The timing of her call to me in the middle of all the legal hassles did not leave me with a good impression.

Ever since Daddy's death, my family has been involved in lawsuits, usually with people who wanted a piece of Daddy's or Mother's wealth. Mother went through a lot of suffering and humiliation during more than twenty years of legal battles. So did Hank, Jr. So did I. It's a sensitive subject for us, and it always means some sort of loss and a lot of pain. Anyone who has gone through long legal fights can understand this. I can understand that Cathy needed to know where she came from. I can even understand that she felt she deserved some part of Daddy's inheritance.

But this is where things get emotional for me. I was Daddy's daughter in his heart, and he was my father in every way but biological. I have never resented that I didn't inherit anything from him. I actually felt lucky a lot of times because my life was pretty normal and I didn't have people always trying to get something from me. But it has hurt at times to not be acknowledged as his daughter. All my life I have had people tell me that they didn't know Hank had a daughter. I have been able to deal with it because I know how I felt — still feel — about him and how he felt about me. Watching the fight between Cathy and Hank, Jr., over Daddy's estate has made me sad, angry, frustrated, and many things that I can't even put into words. It has been twenty-eight years since Daddy died, and the legal battle is still going on. I wonder if it will ever stop.

There is one *specific* gripe I have about Cathy. She never knew my mother; yet, just like all the other people who wrote books about Daddy, she put Mother down. I felt like that was unnecessary and thoughtless. Perhaps she was angry at Mother because of the late 1960s court suit, but all Mother was doing there was protecting the interests of her son. No one could blame her for that. Dale and I tried very hard in our book to be fair to everyone, not to whitewash anybody but to get all the information and be fair. We were matter-of-fact in how we handled Cathy's mother, Bobbie Jett. We did not make any judgments or try to paint her as a bad person. I don't think it would have taken away from Cathy's book to have tried to look at Mother as real person.

I guess I have covered everything I set out to explain. Like I said before, I wish Cathy well and hope that she has found happiness. Daddy would have wanted everyone to be happy. I am, and he had a lot to do with that.

Acknowledgments

We are grateful to the people at Acuff-Rose Music, Inc. of the Opryland Music Group for their cooperation in granting permission to quote from the songs of Hank Williams and Audrey Williams. Special thanks go to Jerry Teifer and Joanne Montella who worked with us on identifying all the copyright details. Following is a list of copyrighted Hank and Audrey Williams songs quoted, arranged in the order in which they first appear in the text. All songs used by permission, made in the U.S.A. All rights reserved. International copyright secured.

"Hey, Good Lookin'," written by Hank Williams © 1951, renewed 1979 Acuff-Rose Music, Inc. (BMI) and Hiriam Music (BMI), pp. 7, 13.

"Baby, We're Really In Love," written by Hank Williams © 1951, renewed 1979 Acuff-Rose Music, Inc. (BMI) and Hiriam Music (BMI), pp. 14, 15, 79.

"Mind Your Own Business," written by Hank Williams © 1949, renewed 1977 Acuff-Rose Music, Inc. (BMI) and Hiriam Music (BMI), p. 18.

"You're Gonna Change (Or I'm Gonna Leave,)" written by Hank Williams © 1949, renewed 1977 Acuff-Rose Music, Inc. (BMI) and Hiriam Music (BMI), pp. 19, 32.

"Mansion on the Hill," written by Hank Williams © 1948, renewed 1976 Acuff-Rose Music, Inc. (BMI) and Hiriam Music (BMI), p. 25.

"Move It On Over," written by Hank Williams © 1947, renewed 1975 Acuff-Rose Music, Inc. (BMI) and Hiriam Music (BMI), p. 29.

"Men With Broken Hearts," written by Hank Williams © 1951, renewed 1979, Acuff-Rose Music, Inc. (BMI) and Hiriam Music (BMI), p. 30.

"Fool About You," written by Ralph C. Hutcheson © 1962 Acuff-Rose Music, Inc. (BMI), p. 35.

"Countryfied," written by Hank Williams © 1951, renewed 1979 Acuff-Rose Music, Inc. (BMI) and Hiriam Music (BMI), p. 44.

"Little Bosephus," written by Hank Williams © 1955, renewed 1983 Acuff-Rose Music, Inc. (BMI) and Hiriam Music (BMI), p. 73.

"I'm So Lonesome I Could Cry," written by Hank Williams © 1949, renewed 1977 Acuff-Rose Music, Inc. (BMI) and Hiriam Music (BMI), p. 77.

"I'd Still Want You," written by Hank Williams © 1951, renewed 1979 Acuff-Rose Music, Inc. (BMI) and Hiriam Music (BMI), p. 78.

"If I Didn't Love You," written by Hank Williams © 1948, renewed 1976 Acuff-Rose Music, Inc. (BMI) and Hiriam Music (BMI), p. 78.

"You Win Again," written by Hank Williams © 1952, renewed 1980 Acuff-Rose Music, Inc. (BMI) and Hiriam Music (BMI), p. 84.

"Why Don't You Love Me?" written by Hank Williams © 1950, renewed 1978 Acuff-Rose Music, Inc. (BMI) and Hiriam Music (BMI), p. 87.

"House Without Love," written by Hank Williams © 1949, renewed 1977 Acuff-Rose Music, Inc. (BMI) and Hiriam Music (BMI), p. 89.

"Help Me Understand," written by Hank Williams © 1950, renewed 1978 Acuff-Rose Music, Inc. (BMI) and Hiriam Music (BMI), p. 91.

"I Can't Help It (If I'm Still In Love With You)," written by Hank Williams © 1951, renewed 1979 Acuff-Rose Music, Inc. (BMI) and Hiriam Music (BMI), pp. 91, 193.

"Let's Turn Back the Years," written by Hank Williams © 1952, renewed 1980 Acuff-Rose Music, Inc. (BMI) and Hiriam Music (BMI), pp. 97, 113.

"I Don't Care (If Tomorrow Never Comes)," written by Hank Williams © 1948, renewed 1976 Acuff-Rose Music, Inc. (BMI) and Hiriam Music (BMI), pp. 101, 104.

"I Lost The Only Love I Knew," written by Hank Williams ©

The lyrics for Hank Williams' songs can be read in their entirety in *The Complete Works of Hank Williams,* which is available from Acuff-Rose Sales, Inc., 2510 Franklin Road, Nashville, TN 37204.

Index

Included in this index are references to song lyrics and photographs in *Still in Love with You*. References to song lyrics are set in *italics*; photographs in the two inserts are referenced by the letters A or B, followed by the page numbers on which they appear.